The Twenty Minute Counselor

The Continuum Counseling Series

THE TWENTY MINUTE COUNSELOR

*Transforming
Brief Conversations
into Effective
Helping Experiences*

Charles H. Huber and Barbara A. Backlund

Foreword by William Van Ornum

Continuum | *New York*

1993

The Continuum Publishing Company
370 Lexington Avenue
New York, NY 10017

Printed in the United States of America

Library of Congress Cataloging-in-Publication Data

Huber, Charles H., 1949–
    The twenty minute counselor : transforming brief conversations
into effective helping experiences / Charles H. Huber and Barbara A.
Backlund ; foreword by William Van Ornum.
        p.   cm. — (The Continuum counseling series)
    Includes bibliographical references.
    ISBN 0-8245-1278-2 (cloth)
    1. Short-term counseling.   I. Backlund, Barbara A.   II. Title.
III. Title: 20 minute counselor.   IV. Series.
BF637.C6H83   1991
158'.3—dc20   90–43296
                                                                          CIP

Contents

Foreword

The Continuum Counseling Series—the first of its kind for a wide audience—presents books for everyone interested in counseling, bringing to readers practical counseling handbooks that include real-life approaches from current research. The topics deal with issues that are of concern to each of us, our families, friends, acquaintances, or colleagues at work.

General readers, parents, teachers, social workers, psychologists, school counselors, nurses and doctors, pastors, and others in helping fields too numerous to mention will welcome these guidebooks that combine the best professional learnings and common sense, written by practicing counselors with expertise in their specialty.

Increased understanding of ourselves and others is a primary goal of these books—and greater empathy is the quality that all professionals agree is essential to effective counseling. Each book offers practical suggestions on how to "talk with" others about the theme of the book, be this in an informal and spontaneous conversation or in a more formal counseling session.

Professional therapists will value these books also, because each volume in The Continuum Counseling series develops its subject in a unified way, unlike many other books that may be either too technical or, as edited collections of papers, may come across to readers as being disjointed. In recent years both the American Psychological Association and the American Psychiatric Association have endorsed books that build on the scientific traditions of each profession but are communicated in an interesting way to general readers. We hope that professors and students in fields such as psychology, social work, psychiatry, guidance and counseling, and other helping fields will find these books to be helpful companion readings for undergraduate and graduate courses.

From nonprofessional counselors to professional therapists, from students of psychology to interested lay readers, The Continuum Counseling Series endeavors to provide informative, interesting, and useful tools for everyone who cares about learning and dealing more effectively with these universal, human concerns.

The Twenty Minute Counselor

Many counselors consider the "standard" fifty-minute counseling session to be a luxury. Because of the demands on their time, they see countless clients throughout the day, in a wide range of situations, not just in the office. School psychologists talk to students in the high school hallway. Therapists who work in hospitals carry on counseling while "making rounds" and may see five or ten patients during fifteen or twenty minutes. Social workers, some of whom have case loads of over a hundred, must make the most of every contact, on the phone or in the field. Priests and clergy hear many problems on the run or in the back of the church. Parents, in giving guidance to their children, must make every minute count.

The Twenty Minute Counselor encourages setting achievable goals, putting them into action, rethinking dysfunctional thoughts, and working actively toward a happier and more satisfying life.

Finally there is a book for helpers that helps them make the most out of all the countless situations when they may have very little time to accomplish a great deal.

The Twenty Minute Counselor helps counselors take an active role with clients during short interactions, in order to help the clients be more active, because "actions provide life satisfactions." Solutions to problems, rather than lengthy analyses of the problems, are offered.

The authors are trained in cognitive therapy, an approach that emphasizes that we can change our moods, our actions, and our lives by making our thoughts more productive.

Flexibility is one attribute that's needed to be a *twenty minute counselor.* The counselor helps the client implement new and more effective solutions. "If at first you don't succeed, try again. If again you don't succeed, try something different," is the idea.

There are many books that emphasize "brief therapy." Usually, this means that counseling consists of a shorter number of sessions. The meaning of "brief therapy" to the Twenty Minute Counselor is that short sessions can have an important impact on the client's life.

The authors present the interesting idea that "exceptions are important." What is occurring when a depressed person isn't depressed? ("Can you think of a morning that wasn't so bad in the last couple of weeks?") When an upset client is calm? By looking at these exceptions, the authors point out how the Twenty Minute Counselor can shed light on better ways of living for the client throughout the day.

This approach can be used with families and couples as well as individuals, and Chapter 7 is devoted to applying the Twenty Minute Counselor to marriages and families.

Readers who are interested in how this approach developed will find an extensive reference list, including work by Albert Ellis, who has been ranked in surveys as one of the most influential psychologists of all time. One chapter includes a full-length twenty-minute counseling session presented in detail; this will help the reader understand how to put the principles of this book into practice.

William Van Ornum, Ph.D.
Marist College
Poughkeepsie, New York

General Editor
The Continuum Counseling Series

Preface
"Briefer than Brief"

In the seventies and eighties the logic of brief approaches to counseling and psychotherapy won the battle for the hearts and minds of many of the young therapists coming out of graduate school and getting their first jobs. Professional workshops and journal articles emerged encouraging the use of brief therapy theory and procedures as mainstream methodology, not just as a "crisis intervention" approach. Traditional rationalizations for treatment obstacles (for example, clients as resistant or not ready for change) began to be challenged by an alternative ideology stressing clients' strengths and resources, as well as a greater responsibility on the part of counselors for successful and unsuccessful therapeutic outcomes.

I consider myself fortunate to have been one of these young therapists (now not as young). I was originally trained in the Individual Psychology of Alfred Adler. I subsequently did a postdoctoral fellowship at the Institute for Rational-Emotive Therapy in New York. These cognitive-behavioral conceptualizations provided a solid foundation for my evolution to "briefer than brief." During the early eighties I was exposed to the brief therapy model developed at the Mental Research Institute (MRI) in Palo Alto, California. It offered a compatible means of expanding the underpinnings of my earlier foundation. Somewhat concurrently, I also became aware of and intensely interested in the ideas and practices being developed at the Brief Family Therapy Center in Milwaukee. My present clinical practice, writing, and research all owe a debt to these sources.

The seeds for *The Twenty Minute Counselor* were thus already sown when I met an exciting and professionally active counselor, Anne Hartman, soon after moving to my present home state of New Mexico. Anne asserted the need for more pragmatic contributions from the Counseling and Educational Psychology Department of New Mexico State University, of which I was a faculty member, to practitioners. As we talked, "time" considerations seemed overriding in her needs assessment. Images of diverse helping professionals emerged: school counselors having only minimal time available for each of the many students seeking their services, social workers similarly constrained by large case loads, community mental health counselors telling prospective clients that they must wait four to six weeks or more for an initial session.

My coauthor, Barbara Backlund, became my research assistant at this time. In brainstorming potential responses to Anne's assertions, the idea of the twenty-minute hour emerged. "After all," we ascertained, "doing therapy briefly does not necessarily have to be the same as doing 'brief therapy.'" Our review of the professional literature and consultation with colleagues revealed that only approaches advocating fewer sessions were referred to as "brief therapy." "Why not brief as to the time allocated for a session?" was our response. We have since spent countless client and supervisory sessions, research, and writing hours polishing this "briefer than brief" approach.

The Twenty Minute Counselor is our contribution to "practitioners"—those who help others—whether professional practitioners such as counselors, social workers, psychologists, physicians, pastors, and others in the helping fields; or nonprofessional practitioners such as family, friends, and colleagues who are interested in assisting those around them arrive at more successful solutions for the difficulties we all find ourselves confronting at one time or another.

Charles H. Huber, Ph.D.
Las Cruces, New Mexico
Spring 1990

Authors' Note

The identities of the individuals in the case studies of this book have been carefully disguised in accordance with professional standards of confidentiality and in keeping with their rights to privileged communication with the authors.

1

Not Just Less of the Same

Traditionally, counseling and psychotherapy have been oriented primarily toward the past. Counselors and their clients painstakingly spent numerous hours searching into clients' childhood memories for the roots of their problems. In the 1960s, the present or "here and now" became the central focus of counseling efforts. Past-oriented psychotherapy was seen by those adopting this present-focused perspective as time-wasting and too speculative. These more contemporary counselors concerned themselves with how problems were being maintained in the present as well as with information about problems that could be confirmed in the present. The counseling process became increasingly time-conscious, with several models of brief therapy appearing. Brief, however, was defined by its contrast with the exhaustive length of traditional models (years) and was still a fairly long-term process (months).

Counseling and psychotherapy have emerged in the 1990s as evolving beyond the "here and now" to a future, "then and there" orientation that is only minimally concerned with how problems arose or even how they are maintained. Instead, counseling and psychotherapy are increasingly highlighting how problems will be solved.

Accompanying this movement toward a future orientation has been an increase in practitioners who are portrayed as being more pragmatic about treatment goals, pursuing aims such as symptom relief and increased coping ability instead of "cure" or basic personality reconstruction. Their practice is based on the premise that psychological change is inevitable across one's life span. All persons encounter difficulties and all possess the strengths and resources to eventually address their difficulties constructively; *counseling is a means of facilitating the time and effort it takes to do so.* Thus, the current belief is that counseling should emphasize and build upon clients' strengths and resources. These counselors further believe that small changes that are initiated in counseling will continue and generalize after counseling ends. Therefore, the "formal" part of counseling can and should be time-limited: "it is more important to be in the world than to be in counseling" (Sperry, 1989, p. 5).

This is a book for practitioners of the nineties about how to counsel with others in order to promote useful change in their lives. Its specific purpose is to identify *what* to do and *how* to do it in the most helpful and efficient manner possible.

Brief Therapy

Until recently brief therapy was generally seen as a superficial treatment approach to be used only in crisis situations or in public mental health settings. Today, however, brief therapy has come to be considered the treatment of choice for many counselors and the clients they serve.

A social worker's case load is made up primarily of women and their children living in shelters for battered women in a large city. Distances across the city are long. Her case load is large. The frightened, tired children cannot sit in a counseling session for more than fifteen to twenty minutes without succumbing to restlessness. Sessions already limited by the growing number of women added to her case load and their limited length of stay in the shelters is cut even shorter by the need to address the most basic of concerns, such as food and clothing, as well as attempts by harried, distracted mothers to quiet their children.

Having been trained in a traditional model of counseling, the social worker described above believes that quality services call for time-honored fifty-minute therapeutic hours with her clients. She is further committed to the importance of exploring and "uncovering" the underlying personality dynamics of her clients, because she believes that presenting concerns are only

Not Just Less of the Same | 17

indications of some hidden dysfunction. She begins counseling by attempting to establish rapport in order to gain clients' trust, confidence, and cooperation. She explains her credentials and the nature and expected duration of her services, works to identify expectations and goals of clients, and then investigates the background and extent of clients' difficulties, including onset, duration, and perceived intensity. She also elicits a detailed family and medical history, as well as information regarding clients' previous experiences with counseling.

While the duration of this rapport-building process differs somewhat among clients, our social worker expects this initial portion of the counseling process to take from three to six sessions, and in some cases up to ten sessions or more. She's convinced of the value of this slow and careful building of trust and confidence for later intervention efforts, which may take an often indeterminant number of additional sessions. She is also, however, becoming increasingly disconcerted by limited accessibility to her clients. Her large case load and the relatively short stay of her clients at the shelters make devoting several fifty-minute time blocks to rapport building a luxury neither she nor her clients can afford.

Following the constructs of traditional counseling models has become impractical for many mental health practitioners. Without the structure of an alternative model, however, counselors are forced to do the best they can given the limitations of the situations within which they find themselves. They attempt to apply the knowledge and skills learned in their traditionally oriented counseling training to the realities of their current practice. Some are able to do so with varying degrees of structure and success. For others, this frequently results in unplanned, haphazard counseling efforts.

How, then, are counselors who find themselves in such circumstances able to resolve these conflicts? Their past training proposes that they rely on traditional methods and fifty-minute hours, yet the realities they daily encounter contradict the value of these practices. It seems clear that there is a need for a therapeutic model that can accommodate a shorter counseling "hour" as well as a shorter duration for overall time spent in counseling efforts. The first step in identifying such a model to meet the needs of both counselors and clients in time-limited situations is for counselors to begin to reconsider their ideas about brief therapy.

Rethinking "Brief"

The adage "Time is money" reflects the temporal mood of the current era. Our culture abounds with microwave ovens, fast food restaurants, and the notion of the "quick fix." One would think that a book advocating a shortened counseling hour would have long ago apeared. Surprisingly, brief therapy as an identifiable counseling approach has so far meant only a brief number of sessions.

Traditionally, counseling has been described as a process continuing for a specific number of sessions (for example, brief therapy equals fifteen to twenty sessions) or for a number of years (long-term therapy equals one to five years). But counseling can occur in the course of a few moments, with only a few words being exchanged. Assuming they are the right words, spoken at the right time and in the right way, clients are quite likely to profit (Sperry, 1989). Embedded in the hallowed tradition of counseling and psychotherapy, however, has been the belief that there is a direct relationship between the length of treatment and client improvement; the longer the course of counseling, the greater the improvement (Fiester and Rudestan, 1975).

Unfortunately, neither clinical experience nor research has supported the assumption that more is better. By contrast, experience indicates that when counselors respond to almost any encounters with clients—even unscheduled ones such as telephone calls or curbside consultations—as potential therapeutic transactions, the outcome is likely to be therapeutic (Sperry, 1989). Research consistently has shown that briefer modes of counseling are at least as effective and sometimes even more effective than longer-term approaches (Perry, 1987).

The matter of perspective appears to be the key element. Traditional counselors tend to have different expectations about the results of treatment than do their clients. Whereas the majority of clients are usually seeking a simple relief from their symptoms, the majority of more traditional counselors typically expect to accomplish more extensive treatment objectives (Beutler and Crago, 1987). Despite counselors' intent, however, the majority of counseling treatments are short (Garfield, 1986). Phillips (1985), for example, reports that the average length of counseling—irrespective of the presenting problem, the setting, or the treatment approach—is only four sessions, with the median number of sessions being only one! In other words, only 50 percent of clients tend to return after the first session.

Some counselors respond to clients' unscheduled termination of treatment with a sense of failure or rejection and question their own competence. Others attribute negative qualities to clients such as "unmotivated" or "resistant." This dissonance between traditional beliefs and counseling reality can be resolved by considering an alternative perspective: collaboration with clients in regard to their needs, expectations, and individual differences. Counselors can tailor treatment to their clients as opposed to expecting clients to accommodate counselors' beliefs and treatment practices. Tailored treatment tends to increase clients' adherence to treatment objectives as well as resultant satisfaction with counseling and the counselor (Beutler and Crago, 1987). Further, by emphasizing the abilities and resources clients already possess, treatment time is significantly decreased (O'Hanlon and Weiner-Davis, 1989).

Counselors open to the perspective that treatment is best tailored to what clients bring with them make optimal use of the strengths and resources clients already possess. These counselors tend to have values consistent with briefer forms of treatment. There are several important value differences that have been articulated between counselors who are oriented to long-term therapy and those oriented toward brief therapy. Budman and Gurman (1983), for example, characterize the values of counselors preferring longer-term treatment as essentially oriented to cure and basic personality change; they believe that psychological change is impossible in daily life without being exposed to the "timeless" quality of formal counseling efforts. These counselors also assume that counseling is benign and useful, and does not have any potentially harmful side effects. Not surprisingly, these counselors view counseling as the most important part of clients' lives and "unconsciously recognize the fiscal convenience of maintaining long-term clients" (Budman & Gurman, 1983, p. 292).

By contrast, counselors receptive to the practice of brief therapy are portrayed as being more pragmatic about the goals of treatment. They emphasize dealing with presenting, not necessarily hidden, "underlying" issues. Coping with life's inevitable struggles is an inherently human endeavor and should be the goal, rather than the attainment of some utopian, stress-free existence. This perspective is based on the premise that psychological change is inevitable across the span of persons' lives, and that counseling can be a catalyst to facilitate and enhance the positive aspects of that change process. These counselors believe that small changes that can be initiated during counseling will continue and generalize further after counseling efforts end. Therefore, counselor-client interactions should be time-limited (Sperry, 1989). Counseling is also seen as a potent change agent that can have harmful or unwanted effects if not properly utilized. Other researchers would add that brief therapy counselors are often more active in the treatment process (Butcher and Koss, 1978).

Among counselors whose values affiliate them with brief therapy approaches are a group who tend to share three other beliefs in addition to those already noted. The Twenty Minute Counselor is a member of this latter group. First, there is the conviction that even a single session or encounter can be therapeutic. Research on client attrition confirms the viability of this belief in planned single-session treatment (Bloom, 1981; Phillips, 1985). Therefore, these counselors consciously approach a therapeutic encounter as if it were the only session and communicate the expectation that change can and will occur both during and after the encounter. Second, these counselors believe that effective treatment can take place not only in traditional settings with scheduled appointments, but also in non-traditional settings with unscheduled sessions or encounters, in a variety of possible formats. Besides public and private practice settings, brief therapeutic encounters can occur in hallways, on the telephone, and even at social events. Further, brief therapeutic interventions can be successfully employed in teaching demonstrations, with groups, couples, and families, as well as with individuals. Finally, effective brief therapy can occur in time frames apart from the traditional fifty-minute hour. The duration of the encounter may range from less than a minute to several minutes (Sperry, 1989).

The Solution Is the Problem

As we emerge from childhood, we begin to press for redefinitions of our family relationships. We may no longer wish to accompany our parents on weekend excursions, preferring instead to be with our peers. We expect to be given an allowance to spend as we wish, to decide for ourselves a suitable bedtime, to listen to music that may be repellent to our parents' ears. We want to borrow the family car, sleep over at a friend's house, pursue interests alien to those traditionally cared about in the family. We challenge societal and family values and traditions, no longer share our innermost thoughts with parents and other significant adults; we insist on being treated as equals. All of this contributes to disequilibrium for youth, their families, and those around them (Goldenberg and Goldenberg, 1980).

The Twenty-Minute Counselor takes the view that we all encounter normal and expected life difficulties such as those described in the preceding paragraph. Such difficulties include sickness, loss of work, transitions in the course of our life like leaving the family home, marriage, the birth of a child, death of parents, and similar concerns, as well as those that might be considered accidents or "just bad luck." For these difficulties to become problems (a problem being defined as a recurring difficulty that has proven resistant to attempts to resolve it), the difficulty is made worse by employing poor problem-solving strategies—unsuccessful solutions. More simply, we turn our difficulties into *problems* when we employ solutions to deal with these difficulties that exaggerate or deny how those difficulties can affect us.

Fisch, Weakland, and Segal (1982, pp. 13–14) address this aptly:

> Our experience has indicated over and over—ironic as it may seem—that something in people's attempted "solutions," the very

ways they are trying to alter a problem, contributes most to the problem's maintenance or exacerbation. We may summarize our point of view of both the origin and the persistence of problems in this way: Problems begin from some ordinary life difficulty, of which there is never any shortage. . . . Most people handle most such difficulties reasonably adequately—perfect handling is neither usual nor necessary—and thus we do not see them in our offices. But for a difficulty to turn into a problem, only two conditions need be fulfilled: (1) the difficulty is mishandled, and (2) when the difficulty is not resolved, more of the same "solution" is applied. Then the original difficulty will be escalated, by a vicious-cycle process . . . into a problem whose eventual size and nature may have little apparent similarity to the original difficulty.

The following example illustrates how one client converted a difficulty, commonly encountered by many persons, into a most disheartening set of circumstances by his "solution" for dealing with it.

Lou was a relatively successful electrical engineer who had risen to a supervisory position in his company based on his normally active, directive way of work. He had, however, become increasingly depressed about his job for several weeks. He was restless, irritable, and had trouble concentrating and remembering names and dates. He withdrew from other persons he worked with. His difficulties began when he inadvertently overlooked a major error in a project he was supervising. His "solution" had been to do nothing, hoping that the error would be overlooked by his superiors as well.

One of the authors saw Lou in counseling after he was persuaded by his family to seek professional help. Lou was able to identify his major goal as feeling more confident about his work situation. He was aided in observing his good and bad times and came to realize his "solution"—a passive, wait-and-see remedy—was contributing to greater difficulty, not less! He progressively was assisted in "readopting" his former take-charge, get-it-done solution orientation, and although he encountered some criticism from his superiors for his error, he was commended for his forthrightness in addressing the problem and seeking their advice as to corrective recommendations.

Such a simple view of difficulties turned into problems may be understandable and yet hard for many to accept. It isn't hard to imagine that people can deal with life difficulties inappropriately, but how can substantial numbers of them not only make such errors but then persist in making them? Such persistence is most often a matter of making logical errors, in a very literal sense. It is not that persons who employ poor solutions are illogical. Rather, it is that they logically employ solutions derived from incorrect or inapplicable assumptions, even when those assumptions don't work in practice. And not only do they employ these unsuccessful solutions, but they continue doing so even after they realize that they're unsuccessful. The traditional slogan for these unsuccessful solution users is "If at first you don't succeed, try, try, again." The Twenty-Minute Counselor seeks to help these persons adopt a more flexible slogan: "If at first you don't succeed, you might perhaps try a second time— but if you don't succeed then, try something *different*" (Fisch, Weakland, and Segal, 1982, p. 18).

Client Position

Counselors may know what solutions would more effectively resolve their clients' problems, but gaining clients' cooperation in the use of these potentially more successful solutions is another matter. This is particularly so, as we have emphasized, when clients' problem-engendering "solutions" are determined by what they regard as the only reasonable, sane, or life-saving thing to do, despite the failure of their solution to resolve the problem. Therefore, getting clients to let go of their own solution and instead undertake some other that they would ordinarily consider unreasonable, illogical, crazy, or dangerous is a vital step if counseling is to be brief (Fisch, Weakland, and Segal, 1982).

From its earliest days, twentieth-century counseling has most often been described as a contest between the forces *for* positive change and the forces *against* positive change. In the beginning at least, clients' problematic behavior was explained as a consequence of their internal dynamics. The counselor's task was to assist clients by uncovering repressed issues. It was expected that when counselors touched on these issues, clients would "resist" therapeutic efforts. The term *resistance* was used to explain in part clients' reluctance to uncover or recover anxiety-evoking experiences. In short, this was the contest: the counselor (for change) was joined in battle against the client's resistance (a force against change). Once the counselor "won" the contest, the client was no longer seen as resistant, and there was a "cure." The problem was solved (de Shazer, 1982).

As counseling models have evolved and become more interactional in nature, the concept of resistance and the term *resistance* have taken on new meaning. As opposed to a resistance that is seen as being "located" in the client and described as something the client is doing, the Twenty Minute Counselor views resistance as a *product of* counselor-client interaction. For example:

CLIENT: My problem has been going on for so long. Other treatments have not helped, but my friend told me that you have been able to help others with my problem.
COUNSELOR: You sound discouraged about yourself and previous treatment efforts. I don't think you need to feel that way. It would seem like our first task should be to determine why you feel so discouraged.

In this illustration, the client expressed an attitude of pessimism, to which the counselor responded with a position of optimism. Despite the positive intention of these comments, they run counter to the client's position of pessimism. The counselor's comments may in fact impede the client's cooperation and a successful outcome for treatment, especially if the client has already been discouraged by previous counselors who began treatment on a positive, optimistic note, only to end counseling efforts with no improvement (Fisch, Weakland, and Segal, 1982).

Considering client position necessitates that counselors take a fundamental stance in their observations and descriptions. Like the ancient Chinese philosophy of Taoism, the Twenty Minute Counselor does not resist the flow but rather tailors treatment to clients' presentations. Taoists believe that Tao gave rise to the "ten-thousand things," and all the many manifestations of the resulting diversity are in a constant flux. This constant "motion" of things is not seen as simply chaotic or random. On the contrary, Taoists firmly believe that this ceaseless process of change follows certain understandable and eternal principles. The spiritual goal of Taoism is to discover and then live in harmony with those natural principles.

The counselor in the earlier example, in order to "live in harmony" with the client, might have made an initial comment that matched that of the client: "I can understand your hope that I will be of assistance to you, but seeing as you've experienced significant difficulty in previous treatment efforts, I think it much more appropriate that you begin with me on the basis of skepticism rather than blind optimism. After all is said and done, results will be the final determinant." By "going with" the client's presentation, the counselor paradoxically lessens the client's pessimism, since recognition of the client's discouragement is directly implied. The counselor does not patronize the client through false hope. Moreover, although the counselor's words are pessimistic, or at least cautionary, the allusion to the possibility of *results* is, on an implicit and therefore unchallengeable level, optimistic (Fisch, Weakland, and Segal, 1982).

By going with clients' presentations, the Twenty Minute Counselor carefully attends to clients' "position," those strongly held beliefs and opinions that clients hold regarding their concerns and treatment. Attending to clients' position provides the information the counselor needs to structure counseling in a way that is consistent with how clients view their circumstances. By working with clients in a way that makes sense to them, they are much more likely to be cooperative (Segal and Kahn, 1986).

Counselor Maneuverability

If the ideal client for brief counseling existed, that individual would essentially present to the counselor saying, "I'll give you all the information you request, in a manner you can understand clearly. I will seriously consider any advice you have about my problem and work hard in trying out the suggestions you recommend" (Fisch, Weakland, and Segal, 1982). It is unfortunate that persons who fit this description seldom come to counseling. Typical clients tend not to comply readily with counselors' recommendations. In our view, this is because they see their current solutions, although unsuccessful, as the most logical approach to problem resolution; counseling efforts are often hindered by clients' fear that their problem will get worse if they veer from their present position.

It is one thing for a counselor to know how best to proceed with clients; it is quite another to have the *freedom* to proceed in the way you as counselor think best—that is, to be able to implement your learned judgment to facilitate counseling efforts. This freedom is called "maneuverability" by Fisch, Weakland, and Segal (1982). They refer to freedom as being a relatively passive state that remains constant, whereas maneuverability "implies the ability to take a purposeful action despite fluctuating obstacles or restrictions" (p. 22). The Twenty Minute Counselor maintains options, shifting or rearranging them as counseling proceeds. This ability to "be maneuverable" is seen as a critical component of efficient, effective counseling.

Traditional counseling approaches tend to view active, directive counselors as taking *too much* responsibility, thus contributing to incapacitating clients via their nurturance of "client dependency." This has frequently been stylized as the counselor being unconsciously manipulative in the form of a negative "countertransference." Although it may appear cold and calculating to traditionalists to consider ways for counselors to control the counseling process, the Twenty Minute Counselor takes the position that persons stuck in vicious, unsuccessful solution cycles simply do not know the best means of resolving their problems. Accordingly, it is imperative that counselors take initial control of the course of counseling efforts. It is important to emphasize that this isn't for the arbitrary purpose of controlling per se. Rather, it is ethically incumbent on counselors to take responsibility for guiding the counseling process, and it is to clients' detriment if counselors abdicate this responsibility.

In beginning counseling efforts, the Twenty Minute Counselor employs certain guidelines for organizing the upcoming process. This normally means deciding which of clients' communications to attend to and which to ignore. The Twenty Minute Counselor endeavors to channel clients' communications to make the best use of them. For the purpose of brevity, in particular, the counselor does not want to attend to comments that will encourage continuing already unsuccessful solutions. Second, also for brevity's sake, the counselor wants to maximize clients' compliance with counseling recommendations.

The Twenty Minute Counselor initiates this process by actively using words that clients use and then channeling the meanings of those words into productive directions or using other words that fit with clients' positions but present a greater likelihood of channeling their actions more productively. For example:

CLIENT: I am at a loss about what to do. I'm just always depressed.

COUNSELOR: What kinds of things have you been doing while feeling depressed? You sound very discouraged.

In this example, the counselor responds to the client's self-description of being depressed by requesting information about what the client has been *doing,* knowing that most persons who feel depressed do very little, a solution that invariably contributes to their feeling even more depressed. The counselor also refers to the client's discouragement, because "discouraged" implies something less disturbed and more amenable to change than depression.

The Twenty Minute Counselor channels clients' communications by translating clients' negative, fixed labels of themselves or others into descriptions of actions. To the client claiming to be an "overeater," the counselor might channel communications in the direction of action descriptions: "It appears that there are many times when you find yourself eating too much." Action descriptions by the counselor depict solutions being employed by clients. "Eating too much" is a solution that can be much more easily altered than a static description such as "overeater."

The Twenty Minute Counselor also carefully uses verb qualifiers as a means of further channeling clients' communications. For instance, when clients talk as if they are "always" experiencing a problem or "never" without threat of the problem recurring, alternative verb qualifiers are reflected back to clients that suggest that at any moment the problem could be resolved momentarily or even completely.

CLIENT: My sister and I are always arguing. A moment rarely goes by that we're not yelling.
COUNSELOR: So your sister and you frequently argue. What's happening during those rare times when you're not arguing?

The counselor's alternative verb qualifier does not presume that no arguments occur; rather they do occur (and frequently), but there are also times when cooperation or at least minimal conflict is present. The use of verb qualifiers can thus be very much a part of creating a context for more immediate change.

The upcoming chapters offer further means by which the Twenty Minute Counselor can use maneuverability to facilitate counseling brevity while helping clients generate more successful solutions to resolve their difficulties. These chapters do so in a manner that attends to client position so as to tailor treatment and thus engender cooperation, not the aura of conflict. The following chapter considers the basis for clients' successful and unsuccessful problem-solving efforts—their beliefs about their difficulties.

2

Thinking ➡ Feeling and Acting

People come to counseling with a set of beliefs that legitimize or validate their previous problem-solving efforts. Beliefs and the problem-solving efforts support and justify each other, and each can be a therapeutic point of entry. In fact, therapeutic intervention will always have an impact on both (Minuchin and Fishman, 1981). Any change in individuals' attempted solutions will change their beliefs about their difficulties, and any change in their beliefs about their difficulties will alter the manner in which they attempt to resolve them.

Beginning clients typically present only a narrow range of beliefs about the difficulties they encounter. They may defend unsuccessful problem-solving efforts that have long ago stopped helping, but as to how they view their circumstances, no other alternatives are possible. They want the counselor to repair and polish their accustomed manner of problem solving and then hand it back to them essentially unchanged. Instead, the Twenty Minute Counselor offers clients different ways of thinking about their difficulties. The facts that clients bring to counseling are recognized as true, but out of these facts new arrangements are offered. Testing the strengths and limitations of clients' present thinking about their situation, the Twenty Minute Counselor builds upon their foundation a more complex view of what is occurring and, consequently, the potential for alternative avenues that will lead to more successful problem solving.

Human Beings

We humans are complex and yet simple organisms. We have innumerable facets that make up our total being. We are constantly in a process of flux as opposed to a static state. We are born with strong tendencies to engage in interpersonal relationships and to live in some kind of family group. Thus it follows that we also have powerful tendencies to be teachable and to easily learn from birth onward the customs and traditions of significant others with whom we live. In spite of being significantly influenced by both hereditary predispositions and environmental conditions that are beyond anyone's full control, we do possess a high degree of potential self-determination. Whether we are consciously aware of it or not, to some extent we choose whether or not to listen to and be further influenced by what we are born with and by what we learn. As we advance in age, we develop even greater abilities to make choices about how we function. Consequently, there is the potential to make changes in virtually all forms of our human functioning.

The Twenty Minute Counselor advances the position that human knowledge is influenced largely by the personal way we think about our life circumstances. This position is derived largely from the creative efforts of Dr. Albert Ellis through his development over the last three decades of Rational-Emotive Therapy (RET). Ellis frequently cites Epictetus, the Roman stoic philosopher, who in the first century A.D. wrote that "humans are disturbed not by things but by the views they take of them." Human knowledge, then, is not considered to exist in any absolute or final form, but rather is dependent to a great degree on human subjectivity—our beliefs about the events we encounter in life.

It follows that erroneous conclusions we take on about ourselves, others, and our world are seen as the primary contributors to human dysfunction. Ellis postulates both biological and hereditary bases for this propensity toward faulty thinking processes:

> I firmly hypothesize that virtually all people are born with very strong tendencies to think crookedly about their important desires and preferences and to self-defeatingly escalate

them into dogmatic, absolutistic shoulds, musts, oughts, demands, and commands. Their very nature is, first, to have probabilities and realistic expectations, and hopes of fulfilling their goals and wishes, and to feel appropriately sad, sorry, displeased, and frustrated when these are not met. But, being somewhat allergic to sticking to probability . . . when they have strong and paramount desires they very frequently, and often unconsciously or implicitly, escalate their longings into unconditional and rigid insistences and commands. By so doing, they create states of . . . "Poor mental health." (Ellis, 1987, p. 373)

We humans are by nature fallible; perfection is an unattainable ideal. Being fallible, we consequently have a natural tendency to make errors and defeat ourselves in the pursuit of our basic goals and purposes. We have an equally natural tendency to correct our errors and move forward in an adaptive manner—to the degree that we have the opportunity to alter our thinking.

The Rational-Emotive Position

The Rational-Emotive position posits three major areas of human expression: thinking, feeling, and acting. All of these areas are intertwined and interrelated, since changes in one will contribute to changes in the others. Thus, if persons change the manner in which they think about their situation, they will tend to feel differently about it and similarly alter how they act. Ellis (1979) affirmed the paramount role of thinking processes in facilitating positive therapeutic efforts: "major change in a person's philosophy can help bring about highly important and lasting changes in both emotions and behaviors" (p. 45).

The Rational-Emotive position places primary importance on *rational* and *irrational* beliefs. Rational beliefs are those that have personal significance and that appraise or evaluate situations in an adaptive, helpful manner. By personal significance, we mean a belief of importance to the holder, not just some passing thought (for example, "My children need to obey me" versus "What a pretty day"). Rational beliefs are also relative in nature. There is no set right or wrong, but consideration is given to every situation as unique and potentially calling for a different response.

When individuals are able to think about their circumstances in a relative manner, they are more likely to experience feelings that indicate pleasure; sometimes they also experience feelings that indicate displeasure, such as sadness, annoyance, and concern. Although these latter emotions are not necessarily desirable, they are considered appropriate responses if the circumstances encountered are negative; they do not significantly interfere with the pursuit of personal goals or, if these goals are forever blocked, the selection and pursuit of new goals. These "helpful" feelings (relative to the circumstances encountered) accompany rational beliefs, which are nonabsolute, adaptive statements of personal significance (Dryden, 1984).

Irrational beliefs are those that have personal significance and are stated in an absolute, unhelpful manner. Feelings accompanying irrational beliefs include expressions of depression, anger, and guilt. These expressions of "hurtful" emotion are seen as going hand in hand with exaggerated appraisals or evaluations of situations and thus are maladaptive relative to even very negative circumstances because they generally impede the pursuit of personal goals. For example, rather than viewing a negative situation for what it is, individuals sometimes see it as much more than just bad: it is the "end of the world" ("My career is a complete failure if I don't get this raise in pay").

Ellis (1982) identified rational thinking as contributing to "helpful" emotions and problem-solving actions, and irrational beliefs as contributing to "hurtful" emotions and problem-maintaining or intensifying behaviors. Walen, DiGiuseppe, and Wessler (1980), in offering observations of their own clients' feelings and problem-solving attempts, agreed: "As long as they remain upset [emotionally], their problem-solving skills [actions] will tend to be adversely affected and their ability to get what they want will be impaired" (p. 22).

The major irrational beliefs people have been observed to hold, contributing to disturbed, hurtful feelings and poor problem-solving actions, tend to derive from a basic *demandingness* or *must.*

1. I *must* do well and win approval for my performance, or else I rate as a rotten person.

2. Others *must* treat me considerately and kindly in precisely the way I want them to treat me; if they don't society and the universe should severely blame, damn, and punish them for their inconsiderateness.
3. Conditions under which I live *must* get arranged so that I get practically everything I want comfortably, quickly, and easily, and get virtually nothing I don't want. (Ellis, 1980, pp. 5–7)

With regard to demandingness beliefs, Ellis (1971) also stated: "Practically all 'emotional disturbance' stems from *demanding* or *whining* instead of from *wanting* or *desiring*. People who feel anxious, depressed or hostile don't merely *wish* or *prefer* something, but also *command, dictate, insist* that they achieve this thing. Typically . . . they *dictate* that life and the world be easy, enjoyable, and unfrustrating; and they *manufacture* overrebelliousness, self-pity, and inertia when conditions are difficult" (p. 168).

Thus, whenever persons begin to feel and act extremely disturbed and upset, the disturbance usually begins with a rational wish or desire that gets blocked or thwarted in some way. The desire is adaptive relative to the pursuit of personal goals, but disturbance and dysfunction come about when the desire escalates into an absolute and thus irrational *demand* (for example, "I must get that raise in pay I asked for!"). Demands can normally be recognized by cue words such as *must, have to, should, ought,* and *need*.

The Rational-Emotive position is probably best known for its *ABC* conceptualization, which describes the interplay between events *(A)*, beliefs *(B)*, and emotional and behavioral consequences *(C)*. This conceptualization begins with an activating event *(A)*. While the commonly accepted viewpoint is that *A* directly leads to *C*, the Rational-Emotive position maintains that the important contributions of persons' beliefs *(B)* about what happened at *A* lead to *C*. Moreover, beliefs are categorized with a focus on those that are either rational or irrational.

For example, the Smiths' eight-year-old son throws a temper tantrum when his parents refuse to take him to a dinner party. As illustrated in Figure 2.1, the common misconception is that the activating event of not being allowed to accompany his parents *(A)* was directly followed by the child throwing a temper tantrum *(C)*. From the Rational-Emotive position, however, it is

Figure 2.1

Common Misconception

A C

activating event   emotional and behavioral
                                    consequences

The Rational-Emotive Position

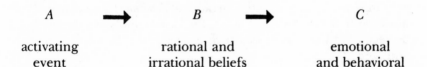

A   B   C

activating   rational and   emotional
event   irrational beliefs   and behavioral
                                          consequences

Figure 2.1. The *ABC* conceptualization of the Rational-Emotive position. (Adapted from Huber and Baruth, 1989.)

the child's belief *(B)* that follows *A* and more directly contributes to *C* ("It's terribly unfair that I can't go. They must take me!"). By contrast, if just at the moment the boy was being told he would not accompany his parents, his belief was "I'd like to go, however, I'll have a good time with the baby-sitter," his response would not likely have been a temper tantrum.

The *ABC*'s of the Twenty Minute Counselor

Taking into consideration the idea that the "solution is the problem" (see Chapter 1) and the focus on persons' thinking offered by the Rational-Emotive position, the Twenty Minute Counselor utilizes an *ABC* paradigm that looks at the recurring difficulties individuals see as their problems as being at *A* (the activating event). At *C* (the emotional and behavioral consequences), individuals experience their unsuccessful solutions behaviorally through the poor problem-solving actions they employ and the accompanying disturbing, hurtful emotions they feel. To change this unsuccessful problem-solution interaction between *A* and *C* requires addressing the thoughts that give this interaction its meaning. This is the *B* (belief). The Twenty Minute Counselor advocates therapeutic intervention that will change the *B* in order to break up the pattern of logic connecting the problem at *A* and the unsuccessful solution at *C*. When that pattern is broken, the problem-solution relationship is disconnected, with the practical effect of eradicating the problem (and solution).

For example, were a husband thinking that his wife did not show him enough gestures of affection on a daily basis at *A* (his problem), he could experience either predominantly rational thinking or irrational thinking at *B*. Rational thoughts at *B* might take the form of desires—wants, wishes, preferences (all relative in nature)—that his wife show him more affection. This rational thinking would almost invariably contribute to his experiencing consequences at *C* such as feeling sorrow, regret, and frustration. These feelings, however, are not those that would paralyze his problem-solving efforts, and thus his actions at *C* would likely be such that he would be open to considering alternatives if his initial solutions were unsuccessful. He would not tend to get stuck in a "more of the same unsuccessful solution" vicious cycle.

Having "relative" desires at *B*, he would likely be thinking, for example, "It's sad I've not succeeded in getting my wife to show me more affection. Perhaps there are other ways I might try."

By contrast, were this man to think irrationally—for example, "How *awful* it is that my wife won't show me the affection I *must have*, I *can't stand* my *abject failure* in getting her to do so, I'm just *totally inadequate*"—this irrational thinking (absolute in nature) at *B* would contribute to his experiencing at *C* feelings of severe depression, low frustration tolerance, and self-deprecation. Also at *C*, his actions would tend to be dysfunctional with regard to adaptively dealing with his recurring difficulty—he might passively give up efforts to explore alternative solutions, or fall into self-pitying behavior patterns such as alcoholism to promote his wife's affection.

The Twenty Minute Counselor posits that when consequences, such as in the above illustration, at *C* are left unattended (by not seeking to change the *B*), the feedback to the original recurring difficulty at *A* is amplified. The result, consequently, is a vicious cycle of "more of the same only worse" problem-solution interactions. This process is illustrated in Figure 2.2. The focus is therefore on rationality as the cornerstone of therapeutic efforts to arrive at more successful solutions.

Relative versus Absolute Life Satisfaction

The Twenty Minute Counselor advocates actions that provide life satisfaction—that is, pleasurable experience for the persons involved. In general, individuals are encouraged to experience pleasure and avoid or eliminate discomfort and pain to the degree that it is possible without inhibiting adaptive goal attainment; to act in ways they believe will help achieve these goals, mindful that this is done within the context of a social world (Dryden, 1984). The Twenty Minute Counselor further proposes that persons actively undertake actions that promise to continue to furnish life satisfaction over time.

The Twenty Minute Counselor, as has been noted several times, accepts the notion that difficulties that occur in the course of an individual's lifetime come to be seen as problems when the difficulty is mishandled, and then when not resolved, more of

Figure 2.2

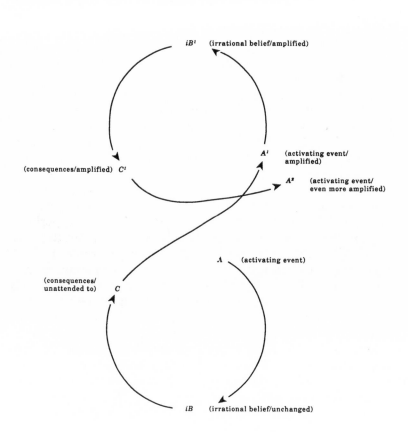

Figure 2.2. Vicious cycle illustrated when the irrational belief *(iB)* is not changed, thus leaving the consequences *(C)* unattended, contributing to "more of the same only worse" problem-solution interactions. (Adapted from Huber and Baruth, 1989.)

the same unsuccessful solution is attempted. Although it may be tempting to assume that rationally thinking persons solve all of their problems, the Twenty Minute Counselor takes the view that these persons encounter difficulties in their lives that may persist, but they do not become paralyzed by "more of the same" solutions. These individuals experience distress and discomfort in dealing with their difficulties. The discomfort experienced by rationally thinking persons, however, is seen by the Twenty Minute Counselor as "good discomfort," which is emotion that contributes to resolving a difficulty and leaves one feeling good about a hard task completed.

The inevitability of change is recognized by the Twenty Minute Counselor. Those who study human development have asserted that all persons go through phases in their life and that transitions between phases are frequently experienced as "crises." While there are some persons whose entire life cycle seems to be an uninterrupted series of disasters, these individuals are relatively rare. Most developmental crises are tied specifically to the tasks required to make the transition from one phase to the next. Thus, a childless married couple who experience contentment may face considerable marital stress with the birth of a baby, contributing to changes in roles, freedom of movement, economic status, and so on. Another set of parents may do an excellent job when nurturing is needed, but fail miserably and see their smoothly functioning family disrupted when their children begin to move out from the confining boundaries of the family unit, as when they enter school.

Each transitional crisis tends to call for new styles of coping. While regression to less effective solutions is always a possible accompanying danger of the transitional stress, the crisis also presents persons with an opportunity to grow by learning more effective coping strategies. Consider the following case illustration:

A domineering, stubborn husband; his meek, child-like wife; and their 16-year-old daughter Joyce were approaching the point in Joyce's therapy in which they were becoming aware that the 16-year-old's repeated running away and sexually acting-out often occurred after father and daughter had had a particularly intense encounter with one another. In their encounters each usually tried to convince the other of the "rightness" of his or her view by means of shouting arguments. When all three came to the therapist's office after a crisis phone call, they began by relating that two days ago Joyce had met a former boyfriend and spent the night with him at the beach without letting her parents know where she was, and had been "raped" by him. The next morning, i.e., yesterday, Joyce had come home sobbing to tell her parents of the outrage that had befallen her. The father was incensed. He didn't believe Joyce's cry of rape; he accused her of being a slut. Predictably, this triggered Joyce, and the father and daughter entered a shouting match. The meek wife spoke up, addressing her husband, "Why object now, it's happened many times before. I don't like it either; but I like it even less that she is getting between you and me again. I had begun to think recently that maybe I was more to you than just the 'child-mother' of your daughter. I don't want her to ruin that." (McPherson, Brackelmanns, and Newman, 1974, p. 83)

A new, more rational belief, and with it a new alternative "solution," had thus been introduced.

Such life events call for change by bringing with them increased pressure and disorganization. This occurs because many of the patterns and regularities that have developed up to this point are disrupted by the new experience; they must be reorganized if individuals are to adaptively evolve in their development. In the broader sense, the continuing life task for rationally thinking persons is to balance stability and change so that they can evolve, without either becoming "stuck" or being overwhelmed by sudden, drastic changes.

It follows, then, that irrationally thinking persons would persistently fail to negotiate these stresses in a relatively successful manner. The label of pathology would be for those individuals who in the face of stress increase the rigidity of their old ways and avoid or resist any exploration of alternatives. When individuals are rationally thinking, they adapt to the inevitable stresses of life in a way that preserves their ability to function while facilitating reorganization of their problem-solving patterns.

When, however, individuals react with pathological rigidity in their problem-solving patterns, irrationality characterizes their thinking.

The Twenty Minute Counselor thus distinguishes between absolute and relative satisfaction in life. *Relative satisfaction* refers to the degree of satisfaction or dissatisfaction experienced by individuals when appraising or evaluating their actions against possible alternatives. *Absolute satisfaction*, by contrast, refers to the degree of satisfaction or dissatisfaction experienced by individuals when appraising or evaluating their actions against some ideal, absolute standard whose attainment is highly unlikely, if not impossible. Absolute satisfaction can rarely, if ever, be experienced, and thus such a goal almost invariably accompanies unsatisfactory life circumstances. DiGiuseppe and Zeeve (1985) term this latter state *disturbance*.

Disturbance is a reflection of irrational beliefs. Individuals' thinking revolves around the belief that unless their life circumstances (or some element of them) are utterly ideal (there is a demand that they *must* be), they are utterly bad (which, of course, is *totally* devastating). Because their life circumstances are not utterly ideal, they further tend to think that they themselves or others are *all* bad as a consequence (and thus are to be denigrated *forever* for their failure). Even further, the discomfort experienced is "unbearable" ("I/We can't stand it *at all!*"). The emotional upset that accompanies such beliefs is likely to interfere with any relative satisfaction that might actually be enjoyed.

Relative satisfaction is a desirable goal and reflects rational thinking. Likewise, *dissatisfaction*, as contrasted with disturbance, also reflects rational thinking. Dissatisfaction may occur for any number of reasons, none of which has anything to do with serious psychopathology, deep-seated conflicts, or irrational beliefs. For example, a marriage that was considered very satisfying when a couple was without children may rationally be thought of as less so when the responsibilities of parenthood impinge on time formerly available for marital pleasures.

Whatever the beginnings of dissatisfaction, it is accompanied by negative feelings that, though intense, are nonetheless adaptive and thus appropriate to the situation. Parents who rationally appraise their children's misbehavior as undesirable and disappointing, and who acknowledge their fallibility, will experience sadness, annoyance, and concern about mutual interactions with their children. They will not feel inappropriately and dysfunctionally depressed, angry, guilty, or panicked. These parents' actions will likely fall into the adaptive range: they will try to improve the situation by various means; or if improvement is infeasible, they will attempt to make the best of an apparently bad situation. Dissatisfaction need not lead to disturbance. Individuals may be dissatisfied with their situation but this dissatisfaction will not escalate to disturbance unless irrational beliefs evolve.

Rationality as the Therapeutic Focus

Most initial counseling sessions begin with clients describing the problems or complaints that led them to seek counseling. Frequently, counselors immediately follow this with an exploration of the complaint in great detail, although what counselors consider important varies according to their approach to counseling. For the Twenty Minute Counselor, this phase is relatively short and takes on minimal importance. Within a very short period of time, the Twenty Minute Counselor begins to focus on when clients are thinking rationally and when they are thinking irrationally. No matter how much a client tells the counselor about the complaint, the conversation is brought back to the client's beliefs about the complaint. The counselor then switches to working with the client to describe circumstances when rational beliefs predominated, thus contributing to times when the complaint was adequately coped with. This is done without getting an exhaustive history of the complaint. For this to effectively and consistently occur, it is vital that counselors maintain rationality as their therapeutic focus.

The Twenty Minute Counselor's position toward rationality as the therapeutic focus proposes two explicit values: *survival* and *enjoyment*. The beliefs persons have can be evaluated against these values in the search for rational thinking. Beliefs that promote these values can be considered rational; those that do not can be considered irrational. Goals for rationality as the therapeutic focus, therefore, might include living life with as much enjoyment as possible given the limitations of the human body and the physical and social world, living peacefully within that world, and relating intimately with certain persons in that world (Walen, DiGiuseppe, and Wessler, 1980). Accompanying these values are several assertions relating to uniqueness, hedonism, responsibility in decision making, and life-style (Wessler and Wessler, 1980).

Rationality as the therapeutic focus values the uniqueness of all persons. Forcing a particular mold on anyone is strongly discouraged. All persons are fallible, and even with the "best" intentions, they are prone to making mistakes. Rationality as the therapeutic focus asserts the right to err, the right to be wrong by any standard, for that is a fact of human nature. Mistake makers need not be valued or devalued for being what they are, unique human beings.

A second important assertion relating to rationality as the therapeutic focus is *hedonism*. Hedonism can be thought of as merely seeking pleasure and avoiding pain and discomfort, but such an assertion would not necessarily lead to *continued* life enjoyment and survival. Deriving pleasure from some action with harmful side effects will eventually eliminate the pleasure. Thus, drugs or alcohol used to excess provide considerable pleasure in the short term but much more pain and discomfort in the long term. Because some short-term pleasures may work against the other main value, survival, the Twenty Minute Counselor advocates moderation.

The term frequently used for this moderation is *hedonic calculus,* a concept taken from the pragmatic philosophers of the nineteenth century (Walen, DiGiuseppe, and Wassler, 1980). Hedonic calculus refers to the evaluation of whether the pleasure of today is likely to backfire in some way in the future. Conversely, if persons lived only for the future, they might pass up a great deal of current enjoyment; the Twenty Minute Counselor advocates noncompulsively seeking a compromise solution that sacrifices neither the present nor the future.

Because humans are unique, fallible hedonists who are mindful of the future, rationality as the therapeutic focus recognizes that persons are faced with continual choices. Decisions are constantly there to be made—some major, some minor, most somewhere in between. Rationality as the therapeutic focus asserts taking personal responsibility for decisions made, with the understanding that choice is limited within the social, physical, and economic constraints of one's world. Ellis (1978, p. 307) offers relevant comment concerning the differences between deterministic and indeterministic theories. He believes that "deterministic theories see individuals as not responsible for their behavior, as pawns of society, heredity, or both. Indeterministic theories put emphasis on self-direction and place control within the person." Twenty Minute Counselors stand mainly in the indeterministic camp. But they see choice as *limited*. They hypothesize that the more rationally people think and behave, the less deterministically they act. But rationality has its limits and hardly leads to completely free, healthy, or utopian existences.

Dealings with others can be based on anticipating the consequences of one's actions. What is rational is specific to each situation; there is no absolute right or wrong. Experience shows, however, that if others are treated unfairly, they will eventually retaliate in kind. Likewise, if they are treated fairly, they will tend to similarly reciprocate. Hence, it would be unwise to exploit and act in harmful ways toward others. It would not be wrong in an absolute sense, but rather in the sense that such actions would likely prevent the attainment of maximum life enjoyment and threaten survival. Thus, decisions about right and wrong are not based solely on moral commandments, but rather on how one's actions affect personal goals, including beneficial relationships with others. Moral commandments can provide helpful guidelines to consider; however, actions are best based on situational requirements and conditions.

Finally, rationality as the therapeutic focus advocates certain styles of living—styles implicit in the notions "It is better to have loved and lost than never to have loved at all" and "What's worth having is worth striving for" (Wessler and Wessler, 1980). "Loved and lost" relates to the benefits of risk taking, not risks that endanger survival but those that might lead to situational rejection or failure. Risk taking accompanies a hedonistic perspective. Maximizing pleasure means getting, as much as possible, what one wants. (Some of what one wants may be gotten without trying; however, the probability of doing so is much lower when left to chance.) To seek to get what one wants means to risk failing. But without risking failure, success will rarely be experienced.

Related to risk taking is the effort involved in taking risks. "What is worth having is worth striving for" reflects the notion that basic values and goals can best be achieved by *actively* pursuing them. Although in some instances the process of striving can be pleasurable, in most it involves discomfort and at times drudgery. Long-term goal attainment almost always requires effort. Wessler and Wessler (1980, p. 61) describe the reverse of this position as being "I shouldn't have to do anything that is unpleasant or uncomfortable, and I'd sooner maintain the status quo than risk discomfort." While everyone clearly has a right to live by this belief, it would likely lead to significant dissatisfaction because it blocks pursuit of longer-term enjoyment and possibly survival.

In summary, the Twenty Minute Counselor advocates a non-dogmatic, nonabsolutistic therapeutic focus that is socially responsible. This therapeutic focus can generally be evaluated by answers to the question "Will clients' actions help them and others or harm them and others?" Rationally responsible acts are seen as those that are both prosocial and proself. In essence this is the "golden rule": Do unto others as you would have them do unto you.

The next chapter considers rationality as the therapeutic focus by looking even more closely at "successful solutions." Successful solutions are seen as the new consequences at *C* that follow a philosophy of greater rationality adopted by clients at *B* in the Twenty Minute Counselor's *ABC*'s of brief therapy.

3

Recognizing Successful Solutions

When a client and counselor meet each other for the first time, there is, as in any initial human encounter, an often confusing mixture of thoughts, feelings, and actions. As noted in Chapter 1, counselors need to make use of their maneuverability and practice a form of reductionism if they are to be optimally effective. The Twenty Minute Counselor structures clients' communications by not attending to some of the information and focusing on other information that they believe will further counseling efforts within the particular context made up of counselor and client. In doing so, the hope of a successful outcome is established.

Though selecting and organizing are required of both clients and counselors, there is one striking difference. Clients are typically demoralized to some degree. Their ideas have not been sufficient, their strategies not adequate, they are experiencing upsetting emotions. As they engage the counselor, they half despair, half hope, that outside assistance can offer them more. In addition, most clients have attempted to resolve their problems through ineffective means, persisting in these tactics despite their fruitlessness. Nevertheless, the very fact that they are now open to seeking assistance suggests their hope—for themselves and for the counselor's skills.

Initially, clients have a kind of "script" they expect to present about their complaint; there is a beginning, and a developmental course, although the end is still in question. The Twenty Minute Counselor structures the client's script within a "solution focus" (de Shazer, 1988). In doing so there is a recognition that there are many potential ways clients can conduct their lives. There is no one "right way," with all else being wrong or abnormal. Accordingly, clients' complaints—their statements of persisting difficulties, hangups that hinder their getting on with life as they'd like to—represent the initial focus of counseling efforts. In certain cases, this criterion may be somewhat modified, but any modification still lies within the same general framework.

Some clients present very vague complaints or grandiose, unattainable, or even contradictory statements of their aims. Even in these situations, the Twenty Minute Counselor seeks to recognize from the available information, unclear or clear as it may be, solutions that would more successfully resolve clients' complaints and help them get on with life. In other words, however questionable or undesirable an aspect of a client's life may seem to us, we would be disinclined to seek to change it unless the client identifies it as a complaint. Correspondingly, the basic goal of treatment is for the client, through recognizing more successful solutions, no longer to have a complaint, or at least not enough of a complaint to seek further counseling (Fisch, Weakland, and Segal, 1982).

An Accident or Just Bad Luck?

Counseling traditionally begins on the basis of a complaint—a statement, sometimes vague and unclear, other times explicit—expressing concern about circumstances viewed as undesirable but persistent. A common assumption of many traditional approaches to counseling is that there are deep, underlying causes not readily perceivable to the untrained eye that cause client complaints. Presenting complaints are seen as "symptoms"—only the tip of the iceberg. Indeed, the very word *symptom* implies that what clients complain of is not the "real issue" but only the outward manifestation of some underlying dysfunction. This iceberg theory comes from medicine, where treating only symptoms can be inadequate or even dangerous. This, however, has been transferred to counseling based on tradition, not empirical evidence.

Continuing with this medical model, traditional counseling and psychotherapy approaches advance the notion that removal of symptoms is useless or shallow at best, and harmful or dangerous at worst, because the symptoms serve some type of purpose for the client's life. They assume that if the symptom is removed without taking care of the purpose it serves, then "symptom substitution" will occur—another symptom will arise to take the old one's place, or the old one will simply recur.

The Twenty-Minute Counselor does not accept the belief that symptoms (clients' complaints) serve some underlying purpose. Prior to initiating counseling efforts, most clients have ruminated over and over again as to the causes of their difficulties. Seldom does this type of analysis aid them in identifying more successful solutions; if it did, they would not seek treatment. Due to prior counseling experiences with traditionally oriented counselors, the ways that movies and television have portrayed the counseling process, or a cultural belief in the validity of a search for causes, many clients offer as their goal for counseling an understanding of "why" they are experiencing their particular difficulty. To this the Twenty-Minute Counselor responds, "Perhaps your complaint came about by accident or is simply a matter of 'just bad luck.' Would it be enough if it were resolved even if no 'why' was ever unearthed?" Generally, most clients agree that resolution of their complaint is what they really want; they just thought they had to understand its cause before it could be resolved.

CLIENT: My life is a mess! If I could only understand why everything has become so difficult for me.

COUNSELOR: What might be one example of the difficulties you refer to?

CLIENT: I'm not getting anything done at work. I hardly spend any time at my office. It just seems so hard to keep up with the workload.

COUNSELOR: You mentioned a desire to understand "why" you're experiencing this procrastination. What I might propose to you is that it's probably an accident of sorts or just plain bad luck. You likely learned by accident that if you procrastinated by leaving the office or coming in late, you could avoid the anxious feelings *in the short term*. This is a common solution, but not a very helpful one over the long term. How about if we

put the "why" aside and focus on taking care of both the long
and short term by resolving this difficulty for you now?
CLIENT: That sounds like a good approach to take.

Strengths and Resources

Individuals involved in unresolved conflicts tend to become ster-
eotyped in the repetitive mishandling of these conflicts, with the
result that they narrow their observations of circumstances to
focus only on their deficits. When they come to counseling, they
present the more dysfunctional aspects of themselves; these are
seen as the areas relevant to treatment. Individuals also tend to
reserve their more competent ways of functioning for those
areas not directly associated with complaint circumstances. The
ways they see themselves and potential alternatives in relation to
their complaint circumstances become narrower and less complex. The Twenty Minute Counselor does not respond to clients'
presentation of dysfunctional stereotypes as if these stereotypes
constituted the whole of clients' functioning. These dysfunctional components are viewed as merely segments of clients' full
potential that are, at this point, most available to the clients'
consciousness.

Many counselors, trained to be enthusiastic psycho-
pathologists, respond to the morsels of pathology that clients
present and are misled into observing only the less competent
parts of clients' functioning. Were they to expand their focus of
exploration, they would find that all clients already have the skills
and resources to resolve their complaints. It is the task of the
counselor to assist clients in recognizing these abilities and put
them to use. Clients only need to be reminded of the tools with
which they are equipped to develop more successful solutions,
or their capabilities need only be honed or adapted in new ways
to assist them in sorting out their difficult situations.

Statements of puzzled curiosity are one manner in which the
Twenty Minute Counselor purports disbelief in clients' presentation of the one-sidedness of their situation. For instance, "Isn't it
extraordinary how you seem to be able to see only one part of
how you can function in that situation?" Or: "Isn't it odd how

you can elicit from your partner only negative, monsterlike characteristics, whereas he seems to present only intelligent and humorous aspects to others?" Clients typically respond to the counselor who questions their pathology with puzzlement or irritation. They frequently emphasize their complaints even more strongly, trying to convince the counselor of the narrowness of their circumstances. With the assistance of the counselor they eventually discover, however, that their circumstances are far more complex and that aspects of competent and harmonious behavior need to be acknowledged to round out the reality in which they live.

Do Something Different

When clients describe their complaints, they usually tell of all the "different" solutions they have found ineffective. A closer examination of these ineffective solutions, however, typically reveals that the majority of them are basically quite similar. Punishment is punishment, whether it is spanking, yelling, or restricting. Thus, most clients are not being different *enough* (de Shazer, 1985). Since they seem not to readily find the different thing to do, they continue to be ineffective in their solutions and they continue to complain.

The Twenty Minute Counselor recognizes more successful solutions by first determining the logic, basic emphasis, or rule governing clients' unsuccessful solutions. By studying these various unsuccessful attempts, the counselor looks for their common denominator as seen from the next higher level of abstraction. Twenty Minute Counselors ask themselves, "What is the basic rule underlying this client's unsuccessful problem-solving efforts?"

Determining clients' basic rule will indicate what might be done to resolve their complaints, but equally important is what to stay away from: recommendations to avoid. Fisch, Weakland, and Segal (1982) refer to this as the "minefield"—those comments and suggestions that are simply a variation of the same unsuccessful rule. For example, the parent who habitually demands compliance from her teenage son would not be urged to become stronger in her demands. This direction would be avoided. Knowing what to avoid, in turn, leads to recognizing what might be more successful solutions.

The easiest way to avoid the minefield and to select a truly different and probably more successful solution is to determine a direction that is 180 degrees opposite the basic rule. Although there are many specific ways in which individuals unsuccessfully attempt to solve their complaints, three basic patterns have been repeatedly observed:

1. Action is necessary but is not taken.
2. Action is taken when it should not be.
3. Action is taken but at the wrong level.

These three patterns of mishandling complaints are detailed by Watzlawick, Weakland, and Fisch (1974). They describe the first unsuccessful solution:

> One way of mishandling a problem is to behave as if it did not exist. For this form of denial, we have borrowed the term *terrible simplification*. Two consequences follow from it: (a) acknowledgement, let alone any attempted solution to the problem is seen as a manifestation of madness or badness; and (b) the problem requiring change becomes greatly compounded by the "problems" created through its mishandling (p. 46).

The second unsuccessful solution has as its premise the refusal to accept any proposed solution other than one based on a utopian belief that things *should be* a certain way. This precludes more modest and attainable goals by insisting on the impossible and making too much of its unattainability. This type of unsuccessful solution based on exaggeration is frequently evident to all except those sharing the underlying utopian belief. Denial and exaggeration of difficulties (underemphasis and overemphasis) are thus unsuccessful solutions that, though apparently opposites, are alike in presenting *extremist* perspectives.

The third unsuccessful solution described by Watzlawick, Weakland, and Fisch (1974) considers levels of change, what are called *first-order change* and *second-order change*. First-order change occurs when clients' actions are different, but these "different" actions are still under the purview of the same basic rule. Returning to the earlier example of the demanding parent, instead of yelling at her son, she might withhold all privileges until he complied fully with her requests. The basic rule, "You must completely comply with my requests," remains attended to.

Second-order change occurs when clients' actions are different and these different actions are under the purview of a different rule. Were the parent's basic rule to be altered (for example, "Some of my requests will be responded to completely, others will not or cannot be"), she might be encouraged to identify times she can commend her son on the cooperation he offers and not come down on him so harshly when he disappoints her. Reinforced more frequently for his cooperation, he could then become less discouraged and consequently learn to cooperate more regularly.

Thus, 180-degree changes in direction to determine "differences that make enough of a difference" would incorporate:

1. Taking action when it is necessary but previously not taken.
2. Not taking action when it is not called for.
3. Taking action on a more appropriate level.

Using rationality as a therapeutic focus, one can characterize unsuccessful solutions as emanating from irrational beliefs (absolutisic and not contributing to life satisfaction). Successful solutions can be seen as following rational thoughts (relative and leading to greater life satisfaction). In the above case illustration, unsuccessful solutions resulted from the parents' initial basic belief or rule that "you must completely comply . . ." (an absolutistic "demand"). Helpful change occurred with a belief characterized by greater rationality (a relative "desire"). Thus, 180-degree changes from unsuccessful solutions to more successful solutions tend to be in the direction of greater rationality in clients' thinking.

Nothing Always Happens

It has been our observation, and that of others (for example, O'Hanlon and Weiner-Davis, 1989), that regardless of the intensity or duration of the difficulties people experience, there are always situations or times when, for some reason, the difficulty is handled well. Parents feel comfortable trusting their rebellious adolescents, combative couples spend an enjoyable evening together, anxious individuals feel calm. Most persons, counselors included, consider these difficulty-free times unconnected or unrelated to the times when the difficulty is fully felt in all its pain and discomfort, and so little is done to better understand or amplify these good times.

There are exceptions to all rules. The Twenty-Minute Counselor defines exceptions as "whatever is happening when a difficulty is being adequately dealt with." This concept is ever so simple. Successful solutions are a part of the repertoire of all clients. Most just don't realize it. They say to themselves, "I must employ solution A or fail." For whatever the reason, solution A seems to them to be the right (logical, best, and only) choice. As a result, other alternatives are lumped together and excluded. These persons consequently become trapped into relying on more of the same unsuccessful solutions because they mistakenly believe that selecting an alternative solution from the rejected or forbidden group would guarantee failure (de Shazer et al., 1986).

How can this happen with such surprising regularity? Fisch, Weakland, and Segal's (1982) explanation of the persistence of unsuccessful solutions offers one likely answer:

(1) From early in life, we all learn culturally standard solutions for culturally defined problems. These standard solutions often work, but sometimes they do not. Since they have been learned largely at an unconscious or an implicit level, to question or alter such solutions is very difficult. (2) When people are in stressful situations, as they are when struggling with problems, their behavior usually becomes *more* constricted and rigid. (3) Contrary to the widespread view that people are illogical, we propose that people are *too* logical; that is, they act logically in terms of basic, unquestioned premises, and when undesired results occur, they employ further logical operations to explain away the discrepancy, rather than revising the premises. (p. 287)

Potentially more successful solutions can be identified by examining the differences between the times when the difficulty is being poorly dealt with and when adequate coping is exhibited. Many clients simply need to do more of what is already working for them. The Twenty Minute Counselor spends relatively little time with clients describing the complaint that has brought them to counseling. Within a very short period after the interaction begins, the topic becomes one of "goals" (" . . . sounds to be your major complaint. How would you like things to be instead?").

After a concrete understanding occurs between counselor and client concerning specific goals sought, conversation shifts to identifying potentially more successful solutions by initiating a search for exceptions—that is, the counselor assists the client in exploring in as much detail as possible those times when the complaint is being adequately addressed or has not arisen. No matter how much a client attempts to tell the counselor about the complaint, the counselor shifts the conversation back to the earlier stated goal and discussion of when the complaint is being adequately coped with and when it does not arise. This is all done without getting a full description of the presenting difficulty or an explanation of its origins (de Shazer, 1988).

Pretreatment Changes

Weiner-Davis, de Shazer, and Gingerich (1987) report the following case illustration:

> A deeply concerned mother brought her 12 year-old son to the Brief Family Therapy Center. For 30 minutes she described, in great detail, the nature of her son's deteriorating school performance and its multifaceted implications. She postulated that her divorce of several years ago had had a lasting effect on him and that perhaps he was experiencing a deeply rooted depression. Just as the therapist was about to consult with the team behind the mirror, the mother nonchalantly mentioned that for the 3 days prior to coming for therapy, her son "had been trying in school." The therapist stopped for a moment, expressed great surprise, and asked the boy why he decided to "turn over a new leaf." At

first the boy appeared perplexed by this idea but quickly affirmed that, indeed, he *had* turned over a new leaf because he was "tired of always getting into trouble." The remainder of the session was devoted to helping the boy determine what he needed to do to stick to his resolution. Therapy goals were accomplished within three sessions. (p. 359)

These authors report questioning themselves as to how the course of treatment might have differed had the therapist ignored the small but significant change that had occurred prior to the initial session. Highlighting and labeling the small change as something worthwhile apparently greatly facilitated the achievement of positive change. Weiner-Davis, de Shazer, and Gingerich go on to report a research program based on these observations, which surveyed thirty families seeking treatment at a rural, community-based organization serving youth and their families in Woodstock, Illinois.

Presenting problems in the study ranged in severity from truancy and "communication problems" to severe substance abuse and the threat of suicide. The procedure was for the receptionist responding to a potential client's telephone call to record minimal intake information, including a very brief description of the presenting complaint. Clients were told that a therapist would contact them later that day to schedule an appointment. The time between the initial phone call contact and the first session was one to five days.

During the first session, after obtaining basic intake information, the following questions were asked:

Our agency is involved in a research project and the researchers have a few questions for me to ask you before we start therapy.
1. Many times people notice in between the time they make the appointment for therapy and the first session that things already seem different. What have you noticed about your situation?
2. (If yes to #1): Do these changes relate to the reason you came for therapy?
3. (If yes to #1): Are these the kinds of changes you would like to continue to have happen? (Weiner-Davis, de Shazer, and Gingerich, 1987, p. 360)

Presenting for therapy in all thirty cases were a parent, typically the mother, and one adolescent child. Of the thirty parents, twenty reported having observed pretreatment changes. All twenty answered yes to questions 2 and 3, indicating the changes they had observed were in, or related to, their presenting complaint. At least in part, they had already achieved what they wanted by coming for therapy. Although the ten remaining clients initially reported observing no differences between their phone call and the first session, most recalled pretreatment changes later in the first session. Case illustrations included the following responses to the research questions:

1. One parent reported initiating therapy because her teenage son was uncontrollable and uncooperative. In response to the research questions, she indicated that for several days prior to the session, he had been helpful and cooperative. He had taken the garbage out without being asked and was fighting less with his siblings.

2. Another parent initiated therapy because of concern over her daughter's relationship with her father, the woman's former husband. The parent was concerned that her former husband's overpowering personality was intimidating her daughter during visits. In response to the research questions, however, she stated observing several days prior to the session that her daughter was being more assertive with her father and that both she and her daughter were calmer as a consequence. Because of these changes, they reported getting more pleasure from work and school, respectively.

3. One family answered the research questions by describing what they had already done to resolve a situation with their daughter's teacher. They reported feeling that their daughter had been treated unfairly by the teacher. Although they had been concerned for several months, they had taken no action until after they called to begin therapy. They thereafter called the teacher and the school principal to discuss their concerns. The parents expressed satisfaction with the outcome of the conference.

4. A middle-aged male presented as having been severely depressed for the preceding four months, following his wife's filing for divorce, which he desperately did *not* want. The situa-

tion had deteriorated to where he made a suicidal gesture. Several weeks later he telephoned for an appointment. He responded to the research questions by saying that he had decided that his wife no longer loved him because he had not behaved "lovably." He reported having been like a "vegetable," sleeping late into the afternoon, not working, crying a great deal, and asking his wife countless questions about her whereabouts. Two days prior to the first session, he surprised his wife with a letter describing to her his new plans to make himself "a better person." The next morning, he awoke at 7:00 A.M., went to school to inquire about returning to his position as a teacher, received information about an accounting course, and indicated feeling better already. He even wondered whether he really needed to be in therapy, since he now knew what he needed to do to resolve his complaint.

One "traditional" explanation to account for these reports of change is in keeping with the work of Emerson and Messinger (1977), who suggest that making a problem "public" by calling in an unrelated third party subjects the problem to redefinition. In some cases, perhaps, the act of seeking therapeutic assistance leads clients to do something different. This explanation has been used to explain the improvement of clients on waiting lists (Schorer et al., 1968).

Another, more popular explanation given for reports of early change in treatment is that the change is only a brief and temporary "flight into health," destined to be followed shortly by a return to the problematic circumstances. Weiner-Davis, de Shazer, and Gingerich (1987) assert that viewing reported pretreatment changes as "flights into health" is a result of the view taken by counselors. They propose that counselors' views directly influence how they respond to their clients' reports of change. For example, a client reporting pretreatment change to counselor A (one who labels pretreatment change as a "flight into health") would not be responded to with a communication that the change is worthwhile. Counselor A would likely ignore the client's report in favor of exploring, in depth, the dynamics of the presenting complaint and the dysfunctional behavior maintaining it. Pretreatment changes are not likely to be maintained, since they are ignored and viewed as insignificant. Counselor A therefore is provided with evidence that pretreatment changes were "flights into health."

Counselor *B* (one who labels pretreatment change as significant), by contrast, would encourage the client to maintain and amplify this change. Traditionally viewed "flights into health" would be seen as real change (although admittedly new and somewhat out of character). Counselor *B* would try to "keep 'em flying" by encouraging more of the "flight" behavior, thereby transforming it into lasting change.

Bateson (1979) draws a distinction between "differences that make a difference" and "differences that do not make a difference." It would seem obvious that some differences might not be different *enough* to be noticeable. The parents who try a new manner of dealing with their child's misbehavior might report that instead of yelling at the child, they calmly lectured regarding what would be more appropriate behavior. Although yelling and lecturing appeared different to the parents, the child might view both as verbal punishment and, therefore, would not see any difference. Thus, pretreatment change that is unrecognized or viewed as insignificant might be a "difference that does not make a difference."

Weiner-Davis, de Shazer, and Gingerich (1987) propose several ways in which "differences that make a difference" can be viewed as promoting more successful solutions: (1) a new behavior occurs spontaneously and there is recognition that something different has happened; (2) in hindsight, there is recognition that something exceptional or different happened, and although the action was not viewed as different at the time, it is now seen as different; or (3) signs of change can be watched for, and therefore anything, any action, or any action noticed for the first time might be seen as a difference. The distinction between "differences that make a difference" and "differences that do not make a difference" therefore lies largely in the meaning attached to the new actions.

To the client who has the belief "This is different," it is simply different. Furthermore, the belief that "This was different" generally leads to the related belief that "Something else will be different." This creates a context within which any new action stands a chance of making a difference. The counselor helps to create this context by asking: (1) What happened that is a positive change relative to how the client's complaint is handled? (2) What did the client do to get that to happen? (3) What can the client do to encourage it to happen again? By implication, the counselor is saying to the client that good things do happen, that the client did something to make the good things happen, and that the client's response to these good things can encourage them to happen more.

It is the belief that there is a difference that seems to make the difference. It is not even necessary that something new occurred recently. Minimally, the actions or events only need to be *seen* for the first time as being worthwhile. The same actions or events could have happened long ago, but were seen in some other context, for example, as not necessarily worthwhile or not necessarily worth continuing. By directing clients' attention to changes they have already made, the counselor's task is a much more efficient one, requiring significantly less exploration and education time.

To uncover those differences that have not yet made a difference (differences that clients either had not yet noticed or that they considered flukes) and turn them into differences that make a difference, the counselor need only ask: "What do you need to do to continue these changes? What might present an obstacle to these changes "sticking"? How might you overcome this obstacle? What could you do that might make things backslide? In addition, since progress has already been made toward accomplishing treatment goals, asking "What further changes are needed for you to feel that your complaint is sufficiently resolved?" offers a clear future direction. Frequently, many clients need no additional changes; they are satisfied to have the present changes maintained for a longer duration, a goal that is usually relatively easy to achieve.

The concept of pretreatment change is a simple one. By incorporating the concepts of "an accident or just bad luck," "strengths and resources," "doing something different," and "nothing always happens," the Twenty Minute Counselor need only assess what is different about those times when clients are successfully coping and assist them to recognize these successful solutions. Clients' "exceptions to the rule" equal successful solutions they have already mastered. Counseling efforts consequently need only focus on increasing the frequency of occurrences that have a track record of achieving (even for very short periods of time) their desired goals (O'Hanlon and Weiner-Davis, 1989).

Chapter 4 outlines the twenty-minute process by which efficient and effective counseling occurs with regularity. Andreas and Andreas (1990), in addressing the current state of brief therapy practice, assert the value of a "methodological approach to briefer than brief." The solution-focused twenty-minute counseling session outlined in Chapter 4 is one such approach to briefer than what is typically seen as brief therapy.

4

Solution-focused Counseling Sessions

The most important area of early inquiry to address with clients is what they would like to gain from counseling. The benefit is that clients' expectations for counseling can be assessed immediately. Positive expectancy increases the likelihood of positive therapeutic effect, whereas incongruence between clients' expectations and the counselor's view of the process significantly decreases therapeutic efficacy. Determining clients' expectations and offering information about the upcoming therapeutic process is particularly critical for the Twenty Minute Counselor.

Clients often view counseling as "pouring your heart out" to the counselor and getting sympathy. Those who have been to traditional mental health professionals frequently expect, further, that their session will be an hour (or longer). Were these clients not apprised that the Twenty Minute Counselor's focus was to be quite different in terms of time and topic, it is possible that significant disappointment and discouragement might follow. Twenty Minute Counselors, especially with clients new to counseling, take care in describing what the process of counseling is like from their perspective and what procedures can be expected. For example:

COUNSELOR: What we'll be doing here may be much different than what many persons have been accustomed to experiencing in counseling. Probably the most important thing we want to focus on is that I believe it's more important to be out in the world than to be in counseling. Therefore, we spend the

60

barest minimum of time "in session." Rather, my aim is for you to consider while here with me some new alternatives to your situation and then go try them out. Our typical time together will be about twenty minutes.

After offering a brief orientation, the Twenty Minute Counselor shifts focus to gather information on elements basic to the process at hand: the nature of the client's complaint (reframed as desired goals), how the complaint is generally being unsuccessfully addressed (unsuccessful solutions), and "exception" times when the complaint has been more adequately addressed (successful solutions). Then the counselor contrasts the unsuccessful solutions with the more successful ones of the exception times and searches for a common denominator or "rule." Interventions aimed at amplifying the previous successful efforts that are unearthed (pretreatment changes) while reframing the "rule" in a more rational, helpful manner conclude the session. All this is done in a clear and explicit manner; that is, the counselor draws out the "facts" of what clients think, feel, say, and do in experiencing their complaints and ways of dealing with them, rather than eliciting global statements or self-defeating explanatory interpretations such as "I'm a loser," "Sue has agoraphobia," or "I lack self-confidence because my parents constantly put me down when I was a child." Concrete, objective data (that is, as objective as is possible given clients' subjective experiencing) are a prerequisite for brief treatment, since they constitute the foundation upon which both effective, efficient treatment can be carried out. Further, rationality as the therapeutic focus predominates throughout the process in the counselor's planning and procedures.

Complaints as Goals

To the Twenty Minute Counselor, much of the information more traditional counselors typically look for is unnecessary. Background information is useful, but following a rigid pattern of elaborate history taking before initiating intervention can discourage client cooperation (Walen, DiGiuseppe, and Wessler,

1980). Some clients feel threatened by so much self-disclosure; others believe that much of the material is irrelevant and that the counselor is wasting valuable time that could be used to help them. If clients are apprehensive about exposing their "real" problems, they are just as likely to hide them during an extensive assessment as during a very short, concise one. The Twenty Minute Counselor assumes that clients will be best served by working efficiently on issues they are willing to discuss. Competence in addressing these presenting issues is more than enough motivation for clients to divulge their "secrets" at some later time. Further, such divulgence frequently becomes unnecessary given what clients learn in more successfully dealing with their presenting concerns. Thus, the Twenty Minute Counselor does not wait for the "real" problems to emerge or seek a list of all of the client's problems before proceeding to identify ineffective and effective solutions of the client's complaint.

To optimize time and effort, the Twenty Minute Counselor immediately ties clients' presenting concerns to therapeutic goals. Following the initial inquiry, "What are the concerns that bring us together today?" with a statement such as "In answering that question, you might want to focus on how you would like to see things differently" sets a goal-oriented tone. Ideally, this goal setting will be a cooperative endeavor between client and counselor. This typically calls for the counselor to be an active participant, not simply a recorder of what clients want to do.

The Twenty Minute Counselor maintains that small change leads to additional changes. Therefore, the counselor should logically start small. When asked about goals, many clients express unrealistic or utopian objectives—that is, what they tend to see as ultimate, end goals. For example:

CLIENT: I'd like to get better grades.
COUNSELOR: What are your grades now and what would you see as a goal for yourself?
CLIENT: I'm getting D's and F's now. I'd love it if I could get all A's.
COUNSELOR: A's are fine as a longer-term goal, but perhaps we might want to consider moving one step at a time. Keeping in mind all A's as an ultimate objective, what might be one or more shorter-range objectives?

CLIENT: I see what you mean. Perhaps moving to C's this coming semester, B's the next, and A's the following semester.
COUNSELOR: That sounds like a fine focus for you to pursue.

Setting goals in increments of small changes allows clients to experience success relatively quickly. Thus encouraged, clients become empowered to make increasingly greater changes in their circumstances.

Another important aspect of goal setting for the Twenty Minute Counselor is that goals should be as concise and concrete as possible. Goals such as "more self-confidence" and "feeling better" are only starting points in coming to some negotiated understanding. When vague goals such as "I want to feel better" are offered, the Twenty Minute Counselor responds: "What will you be doing differently to indicate to you that you are feeling better *enough*?" To illustrate:

CLIENT: I think that if I felt better, I'd be able to get out more.
COUNSELOR: For example?
CLIENT: Well, for one thing, I'd begin exercising more regularly. I belong to a health club and used to go there fairly regularly.
COUNSELOR: How many days per week are you getting in an exercise session at the health club now and what would be an indication that you are feeling better?
CLIENT: I may get there once a week now if I'm lucky. I think that three visits per week would be good. That's how often I typically used to go.
COUNSELOR: So if you were to return to visiting the health club at least three days per week, you'd know you'd be "feeling better enough."

Upon negotiating a realistic and concrete goal, it is then important to get a description of the unsuccessful solution(s) clients have employed in pursuit of their goal (the goal being a more positive reframing of their complaint; the unsuccessful solutions having been attempts to resolve the complaint). Continuing with the above illustration:

COUNSELOR: I can't imagine that you haven't already tried several ways to get yourself out more often, in particular to get yourself to the health club on a more regular basis. What might be some of the solutions you've tried that just haven't been effective enough?

Since complaints are seen by the Twenty Minute Counselor as persisting because of clients' unsuccessful efforts to resolve them, a clear understanding of these unsuccessful efforts is critical. Emphasis is placed on what is currently being done by clients to attain their goal (resolve the complaint). A detailed description of the thoughts, feelings, and actions experienced is sought. When the description is too vague to provide an almost cinematic picture of the circumstances surrounding the unsuccessful solution, more focused questioning is used. For example:

COUNSELOR: When your son begins to act out, openly disobeying your requests, what do you do to try to change things?

CLIENT: I usually try to explain to him the reasons for my request.

COUNSELOR: What exactly do you say? Can you think of an example of the most recent time this occurred?

CLIENT: Just this morning actually. I asked him to clean up his room before school and he just balked at me and continued playing with his Nintendo.

COUNSELOR: You said what exactly and did what next?

CLIENT: I told him that we all have jobs and cleaning his room was his job. When he didn't respond, I began to get more upset and yelled at him, "Get the room cleaned up now!" Then I pulled the Nintendo control from him.

COUNSELOR: And then he said and did what?

CLIENT: He yelled at me to get off his back and just sort of sat there staring at me.

COUNSELOR: And then you said and did what, and how were you feeling at that point?

Formulating goals from clients' complaints and then getting descriptions of the unsuccessful solutions being employed to attain the goals (resolve the complaints) should never be framed as all-or-nothing propositions. The emphasis is on the relative as opposed to the absolute. The Twenty Minute Counselor never suggests to clients that their complaints will be totally resolved, their ideal goals completely attained. Circumstances can be "significantly improved," "meaningful progress toward goal attainment achieved." Likewise, the Twenty Minute Counselor does not suggest to clients that their attempted solutions have been totally unsuccessful; rather, the counselor suggests that these solutions have not been successful *enough,* which is the reason the clients are seeking assistance. This "relative" stance comes from the Twenty Minute Counselor's emphasis on rationality as the therapeutic focus and contributes to clients taking a somewhat more relaxed position toward the difficulties they present, decreasing their tendency to struggle even harder with them, and thereby setting the stage for them to consider potentially more successful alternative solutions.

Exceptions

The Twenty Minute Counselor next seeks to determine what happens when the complaint is not occurring or has only minimal impact on the client's daily life. What happens when the goal the client has identified is being achieved in some manner? Further, what is the client doing to make this happen? The Twenty Minute Counselor maintains the basic assumption that regardless of the magnitude or chronicity of the difficulties clients experience, there are always times when, for some reason, these difficulties are seemingly resolved or only minimally influence clients' lives. Depressed persons feel okay, combative couples have peaceful days, children comply without question to their parents' requests. Most persons, many counselors included, consider these seeming problem-free times to be unconnected or unrelated to the problematic times and so do little to understand them better or to amplify them (O'Hanlon and Weiner-Davis, 1989). In fact, such exception times frequently go entirely unnoticed, their significance unappreciated until recalled in counseling.

As was discussed in Chapter 3, exceptions to times that difficulties are present in their full furor offer a tremendous amount of information about potentially successful solutions. More successful solutions that clients have already proven effective can readily evolve from examining times when the complaint is not actively occurring. Clients frequently need to do little more than amplify what is already working for them in order to resolve even the most persistent of difficulties. They don't necessarily need to learn new solutions, a process that takes up the majority of time spent in traditional counseling approaches.

Clients typically respond in curious ways when questioned about exceptions. They are often quiet momentarily and then appear lost in thought. We think this happens because many people, particularly those whose thinking is predominantly irrational (absolutistic), generally cast their life circumstances in black-and-white, either-or terms: "That child *never* obeys me," or "I walk around angry all the time." Although it is highly unlikely that a child would be able to "never" obey any rule or request, or that a person could be angry twenty-four hours a day every day, this is nonetheless how many persons perceive things. So when clients are asked, "What is different about those occasions when your child obeys you or at least responds more receptively to your requests?" or "What is different about those times that you're not angry or only minimally upset?" the counselor is requesting that clients report on experiences to which they have paid almost no attention. Up to this point all they have been noticing is their child's disobedience, the feelings of anger. They have simply not attended to or viewed with any real significance the occasional time when their child goes out of the way to be cooperative, or when they feel relatively calm and satisfied. As a consequence, they also have given little or no credence to the more successful manner in which they were resolving what at other times they experience as a persistent difficulty.

O'Hanlon and Weiner-Davis (1989) offer comment on clients' frequent surprise at being asked to attend to exceptions to those times when their complaint is not present:

> Another reason clients sometimes seem a bit unprepared . . . pertaining to exceptions is that they do not expect therapy to be a place where one discusses what is going right. Therapy is a place to talk about problems. After all, no TV or movie therapist ever asks about what is going right. In asking about exceptions, we are not only attempting to redirect people's attention to what is already working but also orienting people as to what we think is important to know and talk about in therapy. (P. 83)

O'Hanlon and Weiner-Davis (1989) go on to note their observation that exceptions relative to clients' complaints are "there for the asking." They offer a number of areas of inquiry that we have utilized as Twenty Minute Counselors and found invaluable for eliciting information about exceptions, and with them more successful solutions that clients can employ for the better resolution of their recurring difficulties. (It is important to note here the idea that exceptions are not being sought to identify exceptions per se, but rather to identify situations that illustrate more successful solutions. The Twenty Minute Counselor's primary objective is to unearth these more successful solutions.)

The primary area of inquiry for the Twenty Minute Counselor involves one major question: "What is different about the times when . . . (your child obeys or you're feeling okay)?"

Any difference that can be seen from those times when the complaint circumstances are actively occurring normally provides an illustration of an exception. Initially, some clients find it difficult to pinpoint an exception, but with persistence and an attitude of "You can do it with some extra thought" on the part of the counselor, most clients eventually describe situations during which they are not experiencing their complaint (they are progressing in the direction of their stated goal). To encourage this, the Twenty Minute Counselor assumes a stance suggesting he or she would be very surprised if there were no exceptions. This is done by asking, "What is different about the times when . . . ?" as opposed to "Have there been times when . . . ?" The first question implies a certainty on the part of the counselor that a difference has occurred. Further, the question is asked in terms of clients' expressed goals ("when you're feeling okay," instead of "when you're not feeling angry"). "Not feeling angry" only conjures up occasions related to anger, whereas "feeling okay" focuses on more satisfying circumstances. Occasionally, a client will insist that there have been no times that the complaint has not been present. When this occurs, the Twenty Minute Counselor looks instead to identify exceptions when the complaint was not as bad or only minimally experienced, the "best of the bad times."

Upon describing a difference, the focus shifts to highlighting what the client did to make this difference occur. "What did you do to contribute to that happening?" "How did you get yourself/

him/her/they to . . . ?" "How did you handle that differently from the way you normally do?" On the simplest level, this subsequent focus on clients' different thoughts, feelings, and actions provides information about what clients have done to better deal with their difficulty—a more successful solution.

Contrasts and a Common Denominator

The concept is a simple one: if clients want to experience less stress and greater life satisfaction, they need only be able to assess better what is different about the times when they are already experiencing greater life satisfaction and less stress and what they themselves are doing to make this occur. Therein lies the more successful solution—clients' increasing awareness of those differences that have a track record of achieving (even for short periods of time) their desired goal, and clients' recognizing their personal contribution to the occurrence of these differences (O'Hanlon and Weiner-Davis, 1989).

At this point in the process, the Twenty Minute Counselor and the client have: (1) addressed the client's presenting complaint and reframed it as a goal, (2) assessed those solutions the client is repetitively although unsuccessfully using to seek goal attainment, and (3) identified at least one exception time when the goal is seemingly attained (the complaint is not present or is minimally present), along with the client's contribution to that goal attainment. The next task is to determine the logic, rule, or basic emphasis of the solutions, both successful and unsuccessful. By studying the various individual solutions described, the Twenty Minute Counselor looks for their common denominator and then seeks to answer the question "What is the basic rule underlying this client's successful and unsuccessful problem-solving efforts? For example:

Two parents' presenting complaint was their teenage son's noncompliance. Their goal was to have him obey them more readily. They had several specific "house rules," which if attended to more closely by the son at least two-thirds of the time would offer evidence that their goal had been attained.

In relaying their present efforts at attaining this goal, they reported several unsuccessful solutions: "We've done just about everything imaginable. We've warned him, taken away his allowance and other money privileges. We've grounded him for weeks at a time. We've sat him down and explained that this is our house and he has to abide by our rules. Several times, we've even hit him. We've tried to keep him away from those low-life friends of his who are constantly in trouble by sending him to a private school. He was expelled after a month and a half. We've tried just about everything we can."

"Everything" consisted of variations of the same basic belief accompanying all these unsuccessful solutions: "He *must* obey us" (expressed as an irrational, absolute demand).

To continue with the case example, and moving to the identification of exceptions:

When queried concerning times when circumstances were different, after some reluctance the parents related two seeming fluke situations. One concerned a recent weekend vacation the family had gone on to the mountains. The parents related wanting to have some "together time" as a couple and so they selected a resort where specific attractive activities were planned for children and teens, to allow parents time to themselves. They further reported deciding to let their son "take responsibility for his own enjoyment" and not feel obligated to see to it that he had a good time.

The second exception occurred only the day before, when both were unexpectedly called at the last minute to work at a church dinner in place of a couple who were ill. They described rushing from their home to the church and telling their son he would have to fend for himself for dinner. Upon returning home they discovered he had not only made his own dinner, but also cleaned the kitchen "spotlessly" afterward.

Both situations were attributed to the fact that "he was just in a good mood." In response to specific questions ("What did you two do differently to contribute to that 'good mood'?"), the parents were able to see that they had "backed off" both times. While they still expected their son to attend to the "house rules," they didn't press him about doing so.

As discussed in Chapter 3, assessing clients' basic rule relative to their unsuccessful solutions indicates what might be done to resolve their complaints by suggesting what to stay away from: the "minefield," those comments and recommendations that are simply a variation of the same unsuccessful rule (Fisch, Weakland, and Segal, 1982). The easiest way to avoid the minefield and to arrive at truly different and potentially more successful solutions is to determine an alternative solution 180 degrees toward the opposite direction of the basic rule leading to the unsuccessful solutions. The Twenty Minute Counselor emphasizes the "toward" in looking for a rule that is rational and *relative* in nature, not absolute, and thus the complete opposite of a client's unsuccessful rule.

Returning to the case example above:

"Not pressing" their son (although still rationally *desiring* that he obey) and "demanding that he obey" (irrationally and absolutely) were contrasted by the counselor highlighting the successful and unsuccessful solutions reported and the parents' emotional experience during both types of solution situations. *Demanding* that the boy absolutely obey the house rules was tied to unsuccessful solutions and intense, angry, hurtful emotions. Not pressing the boy, but rather *wanting* him to obey the house rules, was tied to more successful solutions and satisfactory emotional experiences (for example, offering structured situations that allow their son to assume greater responsibility, expecting him to be able to take that responsibility, and feeling relief and pride when he did just that).

Utilizing their therapeutic philosophy of rationality, Twenty Minute Counselors assume that while the specifics of clients' basic unsuccessful and successful rules differ from client to client, unsuccessful rules generally have a strong element of absolutism and demandingness attached to them. More successful rules are 180 degrees toward the opposite direction and have a strong element of relativism and desirousness or flexibility attached to them. The specifics of the unsuccessful solution attempts, more successful exception times, as framed by the goals identified by the client, provide the evidence bearing out this assumption with clients.

Amplifying Successful Solutions

Most clients tend to categorize their unsuccessful solutions dichotomously; that is, in black-or-white, either-or terms. They believe that the only way their difficulty can be addressed is the way it is now being addressed. For example, a husband might blame all his difficulties on his wife. Although this may seem foolish to the objective observer, it is a premise the husband maintains, even though it presently contributes to his significant marital discord (it may, however, relieve him of having to take responsibility for his contribution to the discord). As long as this premise is the basis of the husband's view of his difficulty, and therefore of the way he feels and behaves, then amplification of his more successful solutions is unlikely. But once the husband begins to *doubt* this premise, he becomes open to alternative solutions.

This greater openness is generated through a process of *debate*. Webster's (1976) defines debate as "a process wherein a question is discussed by considering opposing arguments." The Twenty Minute Counselor challenges clients to consider the opposing arguments presented by their unsuccessful solutions and accompanying rule and their more successful solutions and accompanying rule. Once clients' successful and unsuccessful solutions and respective rules have been assessed, the counselor's focus for amplifying the successful solutions comprises three main tasks. The first task is to facilitate doubt about the sanctity of clients' unsuccessful solutions/rule by coupling their unsuccessful solutions/rule with their successful solutions/rule and then compiling disconfirming data relative to the unsuccessful solutions/rule. The second task is clients' exploration of the more successful solution/rule in a way that affirms the greater helpfulness and sensibleness of this solution/rule by highlighting the future benefits. The third task is to review and confirm the step-by-step manner in which the successful solution/rule will be carried out in the coming days. This process offers enhanced opportunity for greater emotional satisfaction (or less dissatisfaction) as well as goal attainment (complaint resolution).

The Twenty Minute Counselor begins debate by highlighting the contrasts between the client's successful solutions and unsuccessful solutions, emphasizing the relevant rule accompanying each. For example:

COUNSELOR: You noted that you do all you can to avoid disagreements with your boss. You mentioned several solutions that have not worked satisfactorily in that you come away continuously dissatisfied. We identified a basic rule that appears to inform all your relatively unsuccessful attempts: "I *must* not argue with the boss." You also noted that the two times you can recall that you were more assertive with the boss, you made your point and came away satisfied and proud of yourself. The rule that accompanied those two occasions, what you saw as exception times, we agreed was something like, "I'd *rather not* argue with the boss, but there are times I will gain by taking a stand." Which of these times are the ones you benefited most from?

CLIENT: When I was more assertive, but the boss was also in a better mood those days.

COUNSELOR: True, the boss was in a better mood, but perhaps your assertiveness significantly contributed to the better mood. The point we need to stress now, though, is would you rather experience the good feelings that accompanied thinking "I'd rather not argue, but at times its better to take a stand," or the depression and guilt that accompanied your thinking "I *must* not argue no matter what!"

CLIENT: The times I was thinking "I'd rather not argue, but it's better to sometimes."

The client's confirmation, even though minimal, signals the counselor to move the debate forward and begin to highlight the successful solution and accompanying rule in a way that affirms the greater helpfulness and sensibileness of this direction. The Twenty Minute Counselor promotes this by facilitating the client in consequential thinking (Spivack, Platt, and Shure, 1976). This refers to the ability to predict the probable consequences of a possible solution. Although having seen the successful solution as an exception time ("but the boss was in a better mood those days"), the client has already experienced success and it is on this success that consequential thinking is focused. To continue with the above case illustration:

COUNSELOR: Based on those times you were successful with your boss when thinking, "I'd rather not argue, but . . . ," would it not be likely that your success will continue if you acted similarly, but just more often?

CLIENT: Possibly. However, I do think much of it had to do with the boss being in a better mood.

COUNSELOR: Well, that may be a second part of your success in dealing with the boss. Perhaps you can look for times when the boss is in a better mood *and* think, "I'd rather not argue, but . . . ," and then act in an assertive manner as you did on the two occasions you reported feeling very good about the stand you took. Given your past success, how likely is it that this method has a better chance of succeeding than avoiding all disagreement whatsoever?

CLIENT: I'd probably feel better knowing I did something instead of backing off.

COUNSELOR: And how will that affect your job performance?

CLIENT: Definitely better. I wouldn't feel so helpless and put upon. I'm sure I'd get a lot more work done.

Once the client has evaluated the more satisfying consequences likely to occur as a result of increasing the frequency of thinking based on the more successful rule and enacting previous "exception time" successful solutions more often, the debate concludes with *means–ends thinking* (Spivack, Platt, and Shure, 1976). Client and counselor review the sequence of events that have been successful in a step-by-step manner. They then rehearse exactly how the client will increase the frequency of the more successful solution and its accompanying rule in the coming days and how the boss will likely react, how the client will react to the boss's reactions, and so on. Typically, role playing or use of imagery is employed to facilitate the rehearsal. For example:

COUNSELOR: We've confirmed that a more helpful thought is "I'd rather not argue, but at times I will gain by taking a stand." I'd like you to keep that thought firmly in your mind.

CLIENT: Okay.

COUNSELOR: Now close your eyes and picture yourself approaching your boss about that memo you recently received on working extra hours over the weekend. Picture yourself saying to the boss, "My work is up to date and I don't need the weekend hours to catch up like some of my co-workers." You've already ascertained that the boss is in a fairly good mood. You're speaking slowly and clearly. Tell me when you get that picture clear in your mind.

(Pauses and waits for the client's response)

CLIENT: I've got it clear.

COUNSELOR: Now what are you saying to the boss and how are you feeling about it?

CLIENT: I'm feeling a bit anxious. I'm saying, "I have something I'd like to speak with you about. I realize the reason for your memo about extra hours on the weekend is for the work to become caught up. I've worked extremely hard during the week, skipping my lunch and and breaks occasionally to keep up to date, and I am ahead on my work as a result. Thus I don't feel it's necessary for me to be here on the weekend."

COUNSELOR: How are you feeling as you state your case assertively?

CLIENT: I'm definitely feeling better, more empowered.

Maintaining and Continuing Successful Solutions

Maintaining and continuing successful solutions amplified during the session can be accomplished by (1) *follow-up,* and (2) *feedback.* The term *homework* is frequently used by the Twenty Minute Counselor as synonymous with follow-up. Counselors do not merely engage in "talk therapy"; rather, they stress that a significant portion of "session time" is best spent outside of session. Clients are encouraged to take what was addressed in the session and regularly use it in their daily lives. "Action" follow-up assignments thus are the major emphasis of counseling.

Follow-up assignments that are action oriented share four important characteristics:

1. *Consistency.* The assignment is consistent with the work done during the session. Assignments should follow naturally from the main theme of the session. Typically, this will be amplification of successful solutions addressed during the session.
2. *Specificity.* The assignment is delineated in sufficient detail and clear steps to take are provided. This should flow from amplifying successful solutions via means-ends thinking; summary/review, however, is frequently helpful.
3. *Small Steps.* Like the goals for counseling, the probability of success is increased if steps are reasonably small and attainable. Small, attainable steps lead to initiation of beneficial cycles of a larger nature.
4. *Seriousness.* When addressing follow-up assignments, it is important to do so in a serious manner. Off-the-cuff or assignments that the counselor presents in a reluctant, apologetic manner, will decrease client compliance. It is important that the counselor review the assignment carefully with the client, including the rationale for it, as understanding increases client compliance.

Feedback is a process whereby clients *verify* the effects of their successful solutions. The more successful solution is implemented outside of the session. Its effects are evaluated. How well did it work? If more satisfactory than previous unsuccessful solutions, self-affirmation is in order. If not satisfactory, what was different from previous times when the solution was successful? Feedback basically involves encouraging clients to be scientific in their examination of results and the conclusions they draw from them (Walen, Di Giuseppe, and Wessler, 1980).

Good scientists gather information as impartially as possible, attempting to observe and report their observations objectively and accurately. Two primary habits that interfere with scientific information gathering are *selective abstraction* and *magnification/minimization* (Beck et al., 1978). Selective abstraction "consists of focusing on a detail taken out of context, ignoring other more salient features of the situation, and conceptualizing the whole experience on the basis of this element (Beck et al., 1978, p. 7). Magnification/minimization "is reflected in errors of evaluation that are so gross as to constitute a distortion" (p. 8). In both types of interferences, clients ignore certain features of their circumstances and thus gather biased information. In selective abstraction, clients focus on one category of information only and ignore others; in magnification/minimization, they ignore information within a category. With feedback, the Twenty Minute Counselor facilitates clients in agreeing on what information is most relevant, thus avoiding selective abstraction. Second, keeping a written account or log of where, when, and how often helps clients avoid the problem of magnification/minimization.

Chapter 5 presents a transcript with commentary of a typical twenty-minute counseling session. This transcript illustrates the concepts and procedures presented up to this point "in action." The commentary is provided to highlight salient considerations as the session proceeds.

5

A Typical "Twenty Minute Hour"

The following transcript of a counseling session is offered as an "action" demonstration of a typical twenty-minute hour with an individual client. The client is returning for a second session with one of the authors (CHH) at a university drop-in clinic. In order to serve students and community people who drop in to the clinic between classes or after work hours, clinic sessions are limited to twenty minutes and emphasize dealing with the presenting complaint. We are grateful to this particular client for his permission to tape-record and reproduce his session in this book.

The client is a recently divorced thirty-five-year-old graduate student. He has sole custody of his two daughters, ages six and eight. The client came to the clinic seeking help to deal better with the anger he feels toward his former wife for her abandonment of him and their two daughters, as well as his feelings of frustration and incompetence in addressing the daily needs of two young daughters. The client's primary presenting concern is his relationship with his daughters. He is feeling overwhelmed by the responsibility of raising two girls on his own. Exacerbating this is his declining performance at his place of work, his boss's increasing impatience with his late arrival in the morning, and the potential loss of job security.

In the initial session, the client offered a brief overview of the difficulties he is experiencing and what he wanted to gain from counseling. His decision to come for counseling was prompted by the suggestion of a friend who had received assistance from the clinic and by the convenience of the drop-in structure of the clinic. The counselor provided the client information concerning the clinic procedures and what might be expected from counseling, particularly from a twenty-minute framework. The client's presenting complaint was reframed as a goal: to improve his relationship with his daughters. He noted that one way he would know he had achieved this goal would be greater cooperation and adherence to a schedule on weekday mornings.

The second session was scheduled for the next day. The counselor's initial statements in this second session begin as a brief recap of the client's presenting complaint and the agreed-to goal.

COUNSELOR: John, I appreciate your coming back to the clinic today. As you know, here at the drop-in clinic we have about twenty minutes to spend together, so let's try to make optimal use of our time. Last time we got together you offered me an overview of what was going on and we agreed on what you'd like to gain from counseling. You mentioned that you recently got divorced and the children, the girls, were living with you. You noted difficulties with that and today we were going to see together how you might resolve some of the concerns that you have about taking care of the girls and developing a better relationship with them, particularly around your morning schedule. So maybe if you could just summarize a little bit for me where you are with that today.

CLIENT: It's pretty much the same as I told you yesterday. Mornings are really terrible. There are just too many things to do and the girls aren't cooperative. They end up fighting and I end up yelling and screaming about things like getting their teeth brushed and getting dressed. Getting myself ready to go to work then becomes a major thing. When this happens, I get frustrated and I just get so mad at my ex-wife. . . . How could she possibly do this to me, leaving me in this situation. . . . She's off having a good time.

COUNSELOR: It's like, "I'm stuck with everything!"

CLIENT: That's right. I feel like I am really stuck, and I'm resentful and I'm having a hard time coping with getting things done on schedule. It seems like every morning when they get up, the girls will fool around. They pick out clothes that are inappropriate. I don't demand that they wear a certain outfit and I try to negotiate. "What would you like to wear?" It often ends up, though, that I think it's too cold or too

warm to wear what they get out, or before we can get going—
and I mean just about every time—they change their minds
and want to wear something else, and its inappropriate and
there's a big fight and I feel like, why can't we just have a little
less conflict so we can get going? It's gotten to where I am late
to work half the time and I'm worried about my . . . my boss is
only going to put up with so much.

As the client recaps his feelings of anger and frustration
concerning his relationship with his daughters, his former wife's
abandonment of them, and his anxiety about his job and his
boss's tolerance toward his situation, the counselor is carefully
considering to himself how this client is rationally and irrationally thinking about his circumstances. In the following interaction, the counselor asks about the children as a means of
focusing the session. He affirms the client's secondary goal,
addressing the client's feelings about his former wife, but seeks
to maintain the client on the agreed-to primary goal: improving
the relationship between the client and his two daughters.

COUNSELOR: Your two daughters, how old are they again?
CLIENT: One's six and one's eight.
COUNSELOR: The six-year-old's name is . . . ?
CLIENT: Mary.
COUNSELOR: And the eight-year-old?
CLIENT: Sarah.
COUNSELOR: You mentioned that you felt really upset with your
    wife and that's something we might want to look at at some
    point, but I think it wise to look at just how things are going
    with the girls right now, because you mentioned that last time
    as your primary goal. That's something you want to see im-
    prove.
CLIENT: Well, that's causing the most problems right now for me.

The Twenty Minute Counselor holds that when clients are
unsuccessful at resolving a present complaint, it is only because
they are trying harder at implementing already unsuccessful
solutions. The counselor asks for a description of a typical complaint time in order to identify the manner in which the complaint is being unsuccessfully addressed by the client.

COUNSELOR: You mentioned that the mornings seem to be a difficult time for you. It sounds like it's really rough and so why don't we get to work in looking at that? Could you describe for me what a typical morning would be for you . . . one that's a really hassled morning.

CLIENT: The alarm goes off at a quarter to six and I get up and make the coffee and usually try to have a cup. Then I get the kids up at ten after six or so. I have a couple of minutes to kind of get myself squared away and then they go in the shower and while they're showering I'm making breakfast and getting their cereal poured or whatever we're having and getting my stuff laid out and getting ready for work and trying to think about what else I have to do. The big hassle usually comes when they start to play in the shower or they don't want to get out or they're still tired and they don't want to get dressed and they want to go lay on the waterbed for a while. I understand that they're just young kids, but it makes me mad, frustrated, and then I start getting angry when I realize that it's already 7:00 and they aren't dressed and they haven't eaten their breakfast yet and the bus leaves in thirty minutes and in the meantime I've wasted a lot of time with them and I still have to finish getting ready for work and be there by 8:00. That's what usually goes on.

COUNSELOR: And you mentioned that you were very frustrated about that.

CLIENT: Oh, definitely! I don't understand why it has to be such a hassle. I mean, I think it's a reasonable schedule and why can't they just do it. I don't know.

COUNSELOR: It was probably a lot easier when your former wife was there because you had someone to share it with.

CLIENT: Oh, yes.

COUNSELOR: And so it is going to be a lot harder now for you, but it sounds like you're thinking, "It's got to be easier than this!"

CLIENT: Yes, I do. I remember when I was married it wasn't like this. It seems to me that the girls just get more obstinate and stubborn and it's almost like I start thinking, "They're just doing it to me."

COUNSELOR: So, it's almost like it's personal now.

CLIENT: Yes. It seems like lately every morning gets worse. The fights get more intense. They start off where they left off and it's getting to the point where it's just intolerable. I mean, I'm really upset about it.

The counselor was not specific enough in his request of the client for a "specific" complaint time. Realizing his error, he requests a *more concrete,* blow-by-blow illustration from the client. The term *specific* as opposed to *typical* leads to the concreteness desired by the counselor in order to depict details of an unsuccessful solution the client can readily relate to.

COUNSELOR: Could you give me an example of a *specific* day as opposed to your typical day? Maybe this morning. Was that a really difficult time for you?
CLIENT: You know, this morning wasn't as bad as yesterday. Yesterday had to be one of the worst days.
COUNSELOR: Could you give me a blow-by-blow description of yesterday morning?
CLIENT: The alarm goes off at ten to six and I get the coffee started and start having a cup of coffee and decide to get the kids up five minutes earlier to see if we can't eliminate some of the time problems. They don't want to get out of bed. They whine, "Oh, we don't want to go to school today." They want to play around, and so I finally drag them out of bed and into the bathroom to shower, and then they don't want to take a shower. I finally get them both in the shower together . . .
COUNSELOR: You're pushing them all the time.
CLIENT: I'm pushing. I'm just chomping right at their backs, and then they're playing, goofing around, squirming, and Sarah dumps the shampoo, the whole thing, right on Mary's head and wastes it all and it's a big mess and Mary starts crying because the soap is in her eyes and she's six, and so they're fighting in the shower and I go in there and yell at them and say, "You guy's get washed off and get out right now and get dressed!" Sometimes, usually if I get mad enough to yell at them and say, "This is it. I've had it!" they will, but yesterday not only did they not, but they kind of laughed, and I really got mad at that.

The unsuccessful solution is the client's determination to "push" the children into cooperation. Angry, irrational demands and insistence on his part are creating tension and anxiety in both himself and the children. They all perform less satisfactorily as a consequence. The client responds by working even harder utilizing a more intense version of the unsuccessful solution. This just leads to further deterioration of the situation and more tense and angry feelings.

COUNSELOR: It sounds like you were also thinking to yourself, "It's got to be easier than this. This is too much!"
CLIENT: I was tired, my stomach was just twisting, it was hurting, and I was just going, "I can't believe this. This is unreasonable. This is terrible!"

In this excerpt, the client restates his absolutistic thinking, which contributes significantly to fostering his continuing unsuccessful solutions. The client's rule seems clear: "It *has got to* be easier!" Now the focus shifts from identifying the unsuccessful solutions and rule to identifying an exception time and more successful solutions and rule.

COUNSELOR: Can you think of a day recently, maybe a morning this week, that wasn't as bad as you described yesterday? Maybe it was a better morning, or maybe a not so bad morning? You said this morning wasn't as bad as yesterday.

The counselor here seeks to elicit the exception time, that time during which the client did not experience the complaint or during which the complaint was less intense or "not so bad." Again, the inquiry is made for the express purpose of identifying more successful alternative solutions and a more rational rule than those normally employed by the client, not just for the sake of seeking an exception per se.

CLIENT: It was still pretty bad.
COUNSELOR: Can you think of a morning that maybe wasn't so bad in the last couple of weeks?
CLIENT: I think that two weeks ago . . . it was a Friday. The girls were invited to a birthday party Friday after school and they

were excited and had been planning on it for a couple of weeks. I told them that unless they cooperated they weren't going to go to the birthday party and I really meant it. They laid out the clothes the night before and they got dressed the next day without any problem at all. Things went so smooth. In fact, we had twenty-five minutes extra, we were ready to go twenty-five minutes early. At five minutes after 7:00 I looked at the clock and they were ready to go to school and they were happy and I felt good. I even felt like coloring a picture with them before they went to school, and we sat down and did that and watched some TV for a few minutes and kind of did some parent-child stuff and it felt good. It was just really different.

COUNSELOR: So it sounds like it was a lot more comfortable for you and for the girls too.

CLIENT: Yes.

The counselor reinforces the positive "feeling" aspects of the interaction. This allows the client to get more intimately in touch with those positive feelings while recalling the exception time. The counselor wants to punctuate that what was occurring during the exception time was different. It was pleasant and desirable and it still feels good to think about it now. The client is thus more likely to be willing to repeat it.

COUNSELOR: You mentioned a couple of things about that Friday morning, but it sort of carries back to Thursday night. You mentioned that you had them set their clothes out on Thursday night. Anything else you did on Thursday evening to prepare for Friday? You also mentioned that you identified some consequences for them.

Clarifying the events surrounding the exception time, which includes the counselor's emphasis of Thursday evening, is important in assisting the client to consider an alternative solution and rule that are 180 degrees toward the opposite direction of his unsuccessful solution and irrational rule.

CLIENT: Sure. I told them what would happen if they didn't cooperate and what would happen if they did. They were

happy and excited and I think they were just in a more
cooperative kind of mood. We didn't have any kind of tension
Thursday night.

Here it is clear that the client sees the exception time as
different only because of the excitement generated by the birthday party. His perception of it as a unique and isolated incident
has thus far prevented him from appreciating the significance of
his use of a different, more successful solution and different,
more rational way of thinking. Therefore, positive outcome has
been attributed only to a change in the children's mood. It is the
function of the counselor to emphasize the change in the client's
way of thinking and choice of solutions and connect this to the
more positive outcome. He does this without discounting the
client's position; rather, the counselor seeks to *add to* the manner
in which the client perceives the exception time.

COUNSELOR: It sounds like they were more cooperative because
of the party, John. But it also sounds like when you compare
that Friday with yesterday morning, or maybe the night before
yesterday morning, you did some things differently than you
typically do, and you were thinking differently than you probably typically think. That Thursday night you set some
guidelines down and did some things to prepare for Friday
morning. You also identified some consequences.
CLIENT: We sat down and had a family talk.
COUNSELOR: What did you talk about?
CLIENT: I told them that it was important to me for them to get
dressed and be responsible in the morning and it was really
hard for me when they weren't. I asked for their cooperation,
and even though I gave them consequences, I turned it sort of
backward. . . . "When you cooperate in the morning, you'll go
to the birthday party." I didn't really have to say if you don't
cooperate . . . It was a good talk between us. I also spent some
time and read a storybook to them, since they were being so
cooperative and were ready for bed early.
COUNSELOR: So you had something that you could use as a
motivational tactic with them. But it also sounds like you
prepared on Thursday evening and I'm wondering . . . You
mentioned yesterday morning was a real bad morning. Did

you prepare for yesterday morning as you did for that Friday morning two weeks ago?

The change in the "night before" routine is emphasized as a successful alternative solution. The counselor also attempts to emphasize that the something different, the more successful solution the client employed, was of his own doing, not a chance occurrence. The comparison with the specific complaint time noted earlier is used to highlight this.

CLIENT: It was a lot different. We ate dinner late and the kids wanted to watch "ALF" on TV, and so we did that, and I got a long distance call and I was on the phone for about thirty minutes with my sister. By the time I got the kids to bed it was late and time to get them right to bed. I said, "Hey, it's late and you've got to get to bed." They were angry about that and they were pretty uncooperative about picking up the clothes and stuff. I had to push them to straighten their room and finally they did it. Then they didn't want to go to sleep and they kept getting out of bed and having all these excuses and I was just so glad to finally have them fall asleep. I was unbelievably frustrated with them.

It is typical of this client, as well as most clients, to have difficulty readily perceiving the dissimilarities in the situations: the fact that the "bad" morning in question was preceded by a disruptive and rushed evening and the "good" morning was preceded by a relaxed evening in which the family cooperated and planned together for the next day.

COUNSELOR: It sounds like you went to bed frustrated and you woke up just as frustrated.
CLIENT: If not worse.
COUNSELOR: John, you said that the night before yesterday morning you were rushed, the girls were rushed. You didn't have time to spend a little quality time with them, read a story, have a talk with them, which is probably a pleasurable thing. And so you went to bed frustrated, they went to bed frustrated. You didn't have time to get things prepared. And so the next morning was very, very rushed.

The counselor summarizes and highlights the unsuccessful solution and successful solution for the client. The hectic, rushed, unpleasant morning was directly connected to the disorganization of the previous evening.

CLIENT: That's normally how it goes.
COUNSELOR: Let's go back to that Thursday evening before what I'll call the successful Friday morning. It sounds like you were thinking on that Thursday evening, "The mornings are rough times and we need to get prepared for them early." You think that's a possibility?
CLIENT: Yes, I think so.
COUNSELOR: So it wasn't like you were thinking, "The morning's going to go easily." It sounds like you said to yourself, "The morning's likely to go pretty hard, but the girls and I can get prepared for it the night before." Whereas it sounds like the night you were rushed you were just thinking, "Well, the morning's got to go easier, because tonight is hard." And it was like, "This is going to *have to* be this way!" There wasn't any preparation and there wasn't very much quality time, no family talk, no consequences.

The counselor repeats the idea that the client's way of thinking about his situation has a lot to do with whether he does or does not prepare for the morning. His irrational rule is contrasted with a more rational rule, which leads to a more successful solution, whereas the irrational rule contributed to the unsuccessful solution.

CLIENT: Yes, and that's the way it usually is.
COUNSELOR: How might you be able to look at your situation in a little different light? You mentioned that that's the way it usually is and that's when you have difficulties. Whereas you just described a situation where it wasn't so bad. In fact, it was quite good and you noted feeling very good about it. It went pretty smoothly when *you* did something differently and those different things were done the night before. But it had a very important impact on the next morning.
CLIENT: Yes, I can sure see that. I think probably by the time I picked the kids up from school at 2:30 they were already preparing for the next day. It was an up kind of experience.

The client recognizes the connection the counselor is making, but still appears to attribute the more successful solution primarily to the difference in the children's attitude rather than to what he himself did differently.

COUNSELOR: What you might want to consider is, "The mornings are hassles."

CLIENT: Yes. They sure are.

COUNSELOR: But add to that thought, "They won't be as bad hassles if the girls and I can spend some time in the evenings preparing for them." Some pleasant time in the evening as you did that Thursday night when you all prepared for your successful Friday morning. The thought you want to keep in the front of your mind is, "If we could just spend a short amount of pleasant time preparing the evening before, the morning will be easier."

CLIENT: Yes. I think it will take a little more planning on my part, barring any unforeseen long distance calls or the like.

COUNSELOR: Sure, those things are going to arise. And even if they do, that might allow for a bit less preparation, or a bit less quality time, but you could probably still spend a little preparation and quality time with the girls, not just for the sake of spending preparation or quality time, but because that significantly contributed to a time you were successful in having the girls respond well to you and they were successful in doing that.

CLIENT: Yes. Sort of like expecting the morning to be hard and getting ready for it instead of just expecting the morning to take care of itself.

The client expresses excitement about his awareness of an already proven successful alternative solution. He conveys his understanding of the more rational rule by paraphrasing it for the counselor.

COUNSELOR: I know you're rushed and that is going to be a continuing difficulty. You're rushed at night as well as in the morning. But I guess if you had a choice, would you rather put in a little more effort in the evening and have a more comfortable morning, or have somewhat of an easier evening and then have things go crazy in the morning?

CLIENT: Well, definitely I would like to have an easier morning, because it really ruins my day when it starts off so badly.

COUNSELOR: Today is Thursday. Let's get together Thursday of next week. If you could drop in again, we could set a specific time to meet if you'd like. In the interim, how can you prepare the evening before? Tomorrow morning's Friday and let's say we get together next Thursday. That would give you about four or five weekday evenings to try this out.

CLIENT: You know, that's a good idea. I'm trying to think of some consequences that might be good ones, because I really think that the party had a big effect on . . . like either offering to do something that they would want to do or . . .

COUNSELOR: John, again, the party probably did have an impact and you're using the party to come up with consequences. That was right on target. It also sounds like another important part of it was a slight change in how you viewed things. Such as, "Tomorrow doesn't *have to be* easy. It's going to be hard and I need to prepare for it." This instead of just waiting for tomorrow to come and saying, "Hey, it's got to be easier!" So changing how you look at your circumstances and following that, getting prepared, spending that little quality time, having a short family talk the evening before . . .

Once again the counselor repeats that the way the client thinks about his circumstances will have an impact on them. The counselor also reinforces the client's recognition of one part of his alternative solution, his use of consequences. This further indicates that the client has shifted his perception of the viability of the exception time solution.

CLIENT: That little bit of quality time and just preparing a little bit the night before . . .

COUNSELOR: And the consequences seem to be real important too. We're almost out of time right now, however, so can I ask you to identify those consequences yourself? I'm sure you can come up with something effective. Please also focus on changing how you view your circumstances differently, as we talked about, and then consequently spend some preparation and quality time in the evening before work and schoolday mornings. How about this same time on Thursday?

CLIENT: Yes. That will be fine.

COUNSELOR: So this will be something that you will follow up on.

CLIENT: Sure, I can't lose anything by trying.

COUNSELOR: I'll look forward to seeing you on Thursday then. I know we're a little rushed in our time, but that's how we work here.

CLIENT: It was nice to be able to just drop in and not have to spend a lot of time.

COUNSELOR: Great. I'll see you on Thursday.

CLIENT: Thanks.

This was a fairly typical twenty-minute hour. The client was able to begin to identify the benefits of changing his way of thinking about his circumstances. As he was assisted in relating more closely to the events of an exception time, he was able to consider a different solution and rule on his part that contributed to success on the morning when things went relatively smoothly. Success here is defined by the client's goal: more cooperative mornings when their schedule is basically adhered to. On these mornings he has positive interactions with his daughters and, therefore, a better relationship with them.

The counselor recommended a third appointment to the client in order both to reaffirm the client's own innate capabilities and to reinforce those changes that will have been made. It is not expected that a further session will be necessary to address this particular issue. It is almost assured, however, that the client will experience other similar difficulties in the future. Some of these he will successfully manage himself; others he may desire assistance with. Because the client has had a positive experience with "brief" counseling, and with the drop-in clinic in particular, it is highly likely that he will return if necessary. His return, however, would be like returning to a family physician for "normal, expected" physical maladies as he and his children encounter "normal, expected" difficulties.

6

Assessing Progress and Addressing Obstacles

Counseling is a process that eventually comes to an end no matter the length of the session or the number of sessions. Sometimes counseling ends for external reasons; for example, the client moves from the area or can financially afford only to contract for a small number of sessions. Occasionally, counseling ends because the client wants to terminate, although the counselor may judge that further sessions would be beneficial. And there are also times when the counselor may decide that a referral to another counselor or relevant professional may be in order—for instance, a psychiatric referral for medication or a legal referral for divorce proceedings. Ideally, counseling concludes by mutual agreement that the client's goals have been achieved.

A critical part of the counseling process, then, is assessing the progress that clients are making toward the achievement of their goals and addressing any obstacles that might impede progress. If attention is regularly given to checking on what progress clients are or are not making, and then giving due consideration to obstacles that might emerge, termination simply becomes an agreement between counselors and clients that sufficient movement toward goal attainment has taken place and that the clients are using the skills and understandings they have learned to maintain and continue on their own (Wessler and Wessler, 1980).

Second and Subsequent Sessions

Chapter 4 offered the primary elements of a solution-focused counseling session and Chapter 5 a case illustration of a typical twenty-minute session. The major distinction between initial and subsequent sessions is that clients' complaints are discussed and reframed as goals in an initial session. Therefore, there is little or no need to talk about complaints in subsequent sessions. After the first session, the emphasis is on these goals. The counselor's initial order of business in subsequent sessions is to focus the conversation on assignments to amplify successful solutions, highlighting the question "What's happened that you want to see happen more?" (de Shazer et al., 1986). This question can be phrased in many other ways and is best tailored to the specific assignment. The Twenty Minute Counselor's responses are those that will detect anything clients can list as worth doing more of, and to identify and comment on them. The counselor's inquiry is addressed to the idea that this former "infrequent exception" is something clients were able to get to recur through their own volition (for example, "How did you decide to do that?" "How did you think to make use of your more successful 'rule'?" "What exactly did you do that you would not have done in the past?").

If clients report that their circumstances are better as a result, the conversation is shifted to questions and comments along the line of "What will you do to get those things to happen even more?" We wholeheartedly agree with the viewpoint expressed by de Shazer et al. (1986): "when something works, one should do more of it or more things like it" (p. 218). That is, the counselor's major objective becomes assisting clients' continued movement toward increasing the frequency of their successful solutions. Further, the counselor seeks to tie feelings of greater satisfaction (or less dissatisfaction) to the client's actions in amplifying a successful solution in order to even more strongly reinforce this positive change.

If clients report that their circumstances are not better or remain unchanged, the Twenty Minute Counselor nonetheless asks questions about what clients did that can be related to their more successful solution possibilities. For example, "It is my experience that if people don't do something right, their situation will get worse, not just stay the same. How are you keeping things from getting worse?" Thus, the focus on exceptions and successful solutions to amplify continues (de Shazer et al., 1986). If clients report that their circumstances have become worse, the counselor would emphasize, "How have you prevented things from becoming *even more* troublesome than they are?"

O'Hanlon and Weiner-Davis (1989) identify three categories of clients relative to the amount of change experienced early in counseling: (1) the miracle group—those clients who report everything going perfectly, far beyond their wildest dreams; (2) the so-so group—those clients reporting things as better, but still not at a satisfactory level; and (3) the same or worse group—those clients who report no change or even regression.

1. *The Miracle Group.* Clients from the miracle group return to second and subsequent sessions eager to talk about the good things occurring in their lives. They are encouraged to talk about their more successful solutions in as much detail as possible so that counselor and client gain a very clear picture of the client's thoughts, actions, and feelings in amplifying successful solutions, and just as important, what is being done that will maintain and increase the frequency of these solutions. O'Hanlon and Weiner-Davis suggest that the question "Is there anything that might happen in the upcoming days or weeks that might present a challenge to keeping these good things going?" can increase the probability that successful solutions will be continued. If clients respond no, fine. If they say yes, the counselor can inquire, "What would that challenge be?" Clients can then be encouraged to describe in detail their perception of the potential difficulty, and plans can be made to address it successfully should it actually arise.

2. *The So-So Group.* Clients from this group begin second and subsequent sessions presenting the difficulties they have been encountering. The counselor should politely but firmly interrupt, suggesting, "Sounds like things haven't gone as smoothly as planned. What have you done to successfully avoid some of these down times?" Redirecting the client's report at this juncture is valuable for several reasons. First, by encouraging clients to balance their difficulties with successful coping times, their perceptions of the difficulties become less pronounced. Second, a critical aspect of counseling is for clients to come to understand that the most direct way to goal attainment (complaint resolu-

tion) is to examine what is working, not what isn't. Some of this group of clients will report significantly increased satisfaction, but will also raise their fear of "easy come, easy go" to shield themselves from disappointment if their circumstances deteriorate. The task then becomes to normalize inevitable "ups and downs." For example:

COUNSELOR: Ups and downs are bound to happen. In the past, how long a period would typically occur between your times of "craving junk food"?

CLIENT: Usually one or two days at the most.

COUNSELOR: You were able to stay on track for four days this week, three days last week.

CLIENT: That's why it has been better.

COUNSELOR: I would wonder what might be considered "success," then? Perfection?

CLIENT: I know that's not possible.

COUNSELOR: That's a rule to consider. "Progress instead of perfection."

The strategy here is to progressively add to the periods of time between the ups and downs previously experienced. Clients can become more relaxed in expecting that their satisfaction will continue and likely increase, but in a rational and relative, progressive manner as opposed to an irrational and absolute, all-or-nothing manner.

3. *The Same or Worse Group.* Clients from this group come to second and subsequent sessions reporting that their circumstances have remained the same or gotten worse. It is important that the counselor does not accept this report at face value without further investigation. O'Hanlon and Weiner-Davis compare this investigation to a courtroom situation in which the attorney objects because the witness is drawing conclusions. The counselor should likewise return to the evidence; that is, inquiry is directed to what specifically has happened as it relates to the complaint and how it was handled. Most often, this description will parallel clients' earlier descriptions of unsuccessful solutions. We typically find these clients stuck in the "minefield."

Returning to their basic unsuccessful rule, tying feelings of significant dissatisfaction to it as well as unsuccessful actions, and then contrasting these with feelings of greater satisfaction (or less dissatisfaction) and more successful solutions of a 180-degree-toward-the-opposite-direction rule change, redirects clients' focus toward goal attainment. Essentially, the process used at the first session is repeated. Occasionally, in approaching second or subsequent sessions in which clients report their circumstances not changing or getting worse, it is valuable for counselors to examine themselves and the manner in which counseling is being pursued. Is the counselor and counseling part of the problem instead of part of a more successful solution? Just as clients repeat unsuccessful solutions, counselors sometimes do so as well (recommendations for handling this type of problem are made later in this chapter). Finally, if clients' circumstances remain the same or progressively worsen, referral to another practitioner is in order. Perhaps another counselor will come up with a greater number of alternative solutions to consider with the client. Such a referral can be a successful solution to pursue when all else has only produced "more of the same."

Assessing Therapeutic Progress

Counseling of any kind usually begins on the basis of a complaint—a statement, more or less clear and explicit, expressing concern about circumstances that the presenter views as undesirable and persistent. Most traditional approaches to counseling and psychotherapy, however, soon depart from this starting point, never to return. They shift to something viewed as deeper and more significant than the client's presenting complaint—some underlying pathology or presumed cause. Correspondingly, with these approaches, goals are formulated and progress assessed in accordance with some explicit or implied concept of "health" or "normality" (Fisch, Weakland, and Segal, 1982).

In our view, there are many possible ways individuals can live normal, healthy lives, rather than one static standard, with any deviation from that standard considered maladaptive or abnormal. Accordingly, clients' complaints—their statement of persistent difficulties, hangups that hinder getting on with life as they wish to pursue it—are the primary focus throughout counseling. In some instances, a client's goal may need to be modified (for example, when pursuit of the goal as stated might occasion harm to self or others), but the modification would be one that still lies within this same general framework (a reframing of the same goal so that it might be achieved without harm to self or others).

Given this caveat, the most important indicator of successful treatment is a client's *statement* of contentment with the progress of counseling—either because the goal agreed to was achieved (complaint resolved) or because the client's perception of the complaint has changed, and it is no longer seen as a significant difficulty. The emphasis, therefore, is on the client's report as the primary index of success: a client who enters counseling as a complainant should leave as a noncomplainant. We do in addition, however, attempt to substantiate the client's report in several ways.

First, from our own observations during the course of counseling efforts, we regularly ask ourselves, "To what degree is this client: (1) utilizing successful solutions identified from exception times; (2) considering the more helpful rule accompanying these more successful solutions; and (3) moving toward a position of greater rationality?" Second, as clients begin to report movement from a complainant to noncomplainant position, we inquire, "What has happened to account for the changes you see?" Again, the main criteria used are reports that indicate a "shift" to utilizing more successful solutions, greater consideration of the more helpful rule accompanying these successful solutions, and a position of increased rationality. In assessing both our own observations and clients' reports, it is critical that clients are actively *doing* some things more consistently than they had before. With a client who had presented as depressed, we would be more interested in hearing that the client had begun a daily exercise program than that the client "felt better because the weather's become sunny and warmer."

Similarly, when complaint circumstances have not changed but the client no longer regards them as a significant difficulty, we do not necessarily consider a sign of therapeutic progress the statement, "I don't think I need to continue counseling. My problem's not so bad anymore." Rather, we prefer to hear clients *redefine* their presenting complaint as no longer a significant difficulty. For example:

CLIENT: I have always been so concerned about how many friends I have or, really, don't have. The last few years especially have just been a litany of efforts aimed at pleasing others. I've come to realize that I've been more miserable because I've ignored my own desires as a result. I've decided that the most important person in my life is me and I can enjoy my own company and not feel guilty or panicked when I'm alone. That doesn't mean I don't want to be with others, just that I don't have to exert all of my efforts on others. Therefore, I don't think that I need to continue counseling right now.

While the client's goal of having more friends has not been attained (the complaint of not having enough friends has not literally been resolved), there has been a *qualitative shift*. Although the client does not explicitly express it, the utilization of more successful solutions, consideration of a more helpful rule, and a position of greater rationality are all evident in the above statement.

Client Obstacles

All clients do not make the progress they and their counselor might desire. Some clients simply present certain difficulties or display certain characteristics that interfere with their progress in counseling. Specifically, the majority of this interference occurs when clients become "stuck." They irrationally and absolutistically perceive their difficulties as intractable or themselves as intractable because they are unable to have a more successful impact on the difficulties.

De Shazer and Molnar (1984) address client "stuckness" in identifying three obstacles frequently presented by clients in their brief therapy practice. They also suggest interventions aimed at assisting clients *experience* their successful solutions more succinctly so that they are attended to and able to be replicated. We have utilized variations of these interventions and found them particularly appropriate in facilitating client movement toward greater rationality and openness to alternative solutions.

Client obstacle 1 is presented by those clients who focus on the perceived stability of their complaint. These clients offer a pessimistic view that nothing worthwhile can come of their circumstances. The primary intervention here is to communicate to the client a message akin to: "Between now and the next time we meet, I want you to observe what has happened in your life that you want to continue to happen." This message defines the client's circumstances as those in which the counselor expects worthwhile occurrences to happen. This is typically the opposite of what the client is expecting, which is that circumstances will remain static.

To further promote these expectations and to assist the client in more readily perceiving these worthwhile occurrences, the counselor carefully opens the next session with the question "So, what exactly happened that you want to continue to happen?" The counselor then responds to any of the information the client provides with comments that reinforce, however minimally, the client's more successful solution behaviors. The primary purpose here, then, is progressively to build a foundation by which clients can see exceptions and recognize their impact on the more successful solutions that occur. Consider the following case illustration:

> A husband presented with the complaint that his wife "lived for" their three, now adult, daughters. He noted that this had been acceptable to him when the daughters were younger, but now that they were out of the family home, he expected more attention from his wife. He spent the first session describing her devotion to the daughters and "total disregard" of him. The counselor's efforts to have him identify exception times when his wife attended to him, even minimally, were unsuccessful. In response to the request that he observe what had happened in his life over the previous week that he'd like to see continue, the husband reported that his wife had gone out to dinner with him and talked about him and his work while at dinner. This opened the door for the counselor to suggest

that the husband's actions had facilitated these desired occurrences. Further discussion revealed that the husband's unsuccessful solution orientation was to expect his wife to spontaneously increase the attention she showed him. Investigation into the dinner and conversation they had had the previous week indicated that he had initiated both occurrences. He did not wait for her spontaneously to invite him to dinner or to begin to discuss his work.

The message "Observe what has happened in your life that you want to continue to happen" does not "cause" worthwhile things to occur. As in the case illustration above, it simply affects clients' expectations in such a manner that they pay greater attention to and then report worthwhile things in their daily lives. Once these exception times are noted, counseling can move forward readily.

Client obstacle 2 is presented by clients who believe that they have used up all possible responses in trying to resolve their complaint. These clients tend to complain about a sequence of events that continually repeats itself. In responding to these events their range of possible solutions is limited by what they think is correct, moral, or logical. The intervention here is to request that the client simply "do something different."

This direct, nonspecific intervention gives clients a wide range of possible solutions to choose from and ensures that, when they do something different, it will be something that fits for them and not something specifically suggested by the counselor that might seem outside the bounds of possibility for them (de Shazer and Molnar, 1984). For example:

Two parents complained that their eleven-year old son was "uncontrollable." The parents were both college educated and, as they described, "well read in parenting strategies." They reported being firm adherents of "positive parenting" methods that had been relatively successful until about two years ago, when signs of opposition began to appear regularly. At the end of the initial session, the counselor said to them, "Before we meet next, do something different when your son acts in opposition to any reasonable request you make. No matter how strange or weird something you do might seem, the important thing is that whatever you decide to do, make it different from your normal response." Two days later, the son began to talk back to his mother in response to her request that he straighten up his room. The father, who had just come home from an extremely difficult day, heard his son's refusal and suddenly decided it was time that the boy find out what the real world was like. The father entered the boy's room and began to yell and "read him the riot act." He even suggested that the boy was due a spanking. The boy, apparently shocked by his father's anger, immediately apologized to both parents and proceeded to clean his room. The parents reported the rest of the week went very well with him.

In this case example, the father's anger was effective because it was not "more of the same" unsuccessful solution pattern of "positive parenting" that the parents had been irrationally and perfectionistically adhering to. The point here is not that "positive parenting" is inappropriate or wrong (more likely, it is an ideal approach for most parents), rather it simply was a solution pattern that was not working satisfactorily and the parents kept repeating it nonetheless. The presentation of anger was a more successful solution for the very reason that it was "different enough." The show of anger allowed the boy to experience negative consequences for his negative behavior, a prerequisite if he is to be able to differentiate and thus enjoy the positive consequences offered for his positive behavior. For counseling purposes, it offered an exception time when a more successful solution was realized—a solution upon which subsequent counseling efforts can build.

Client obstacle 3 is presented by clients who tend to view their complaint as compulsive and beyond their control. The intervention that should be communicated to clients offering this obstacle is: "Before we meet next, pay attention to what you do to overcome the temptation or urge to . . ." This intervention is a combination of that suggested with regard to both client obstacle 1 and client obstacle 2; it presupposes that clients *will* overcome their temptations or urges at least some of the time, and that they will do something different from their normal response in order to overcome them (de Shazer and Molnar, 1984).

In the session subsequent to the assignment of this task, the counselor begins with a comment such as "What did you do when you overcame your urge to . . . since we last met?" Regardless of the degree of success clients report experiencing, they are then encouraged to see this as an exception time, incorporating a successful solution with counseling efforts proceeding from that point as described for a first session. The following case is offered as an example of a response to client obstacle 3:

> A young woman initially presented as binging on large quantities of cookies, donuts, and ice cream daily described her consumption of these as beyond her control. She noted simply going to the supermarket or a specialty shop whenever the urge struck. At the beginning of the session subsequent to being asked to "pay attention to what you do to overcome the temptation to binge," the client reported experiencing the urge to binge at break time at her job but then realizing that she had no money and no time to get to the automatic teller before she was due back at her work station. She and the counselor were thereafter able to progress with counseling efforts by building upon this "successful solution" of not carrying money with her when she might experience the urge to binge.

Counselor Obstacles

It is often tempting to attribute to the client responsibility for lack of progress in counseling. The term *client resistance* epitomizes the placing of fault directly on and within the client. Although client obstacles can impede counseling progress, as just discussed, the counselor can also contribute to a lack of progress. Since the counselor, as expert provider of therapeutic services, has the major responsibility for the structure of counseling efforts, lack of progress may be due to the counselor's unsuccessful manner of facilitating this structure. O'Hanlon and Weiner-Davis (1989) describe several traps into which counselors they supervise frequently stumble. They note in this regard: "If the therapist stays on the road to solution, all is well. However when he or she strays off the main road, therapy can go in unproductive directions, become mired in the swamp of pathology, or follow dead-end roads with no solutions in sight" (p. 163).

Following the work of O'Hanlon and Weiner-Davis, our experience has been that counselors, like clients, tend to encounter three major obstacles: (1) poor goal-setting practices, (2) repetition of unsuccessful solutions, and (3) a search for problems instead of solutions.

Counselor obstacle 1 occurs when counselors do not keep the importance of treatment goals foremost in their minds. This is a major obstacle to counseling efforts, because if counselors don't know where they and their clients are going, how will they together know when they get there? How will they know if they're even headed in the right direction? Typically, when this obstacle is present, the counselor has never had a clear picture of the client's goal. The goal may have been stated in vague or attitudinal terms, as opposed to observable actions (for example, "I will feel happier" rather than "I will go out more often with friends"). Since attitudes such as "feeling happier" can't be seen, it becomes difficult for both the counselor and client to know when they are happening, let alone happening sufficiently. It is not unusual, therefore, for both counselor and client to think they are going around in circles; likely they are (O'Hanlon and Weiner-Davis, 1989).

Some counselors begin working with clients by reframing complaints into concrete and observable goals. Counselor obstacle 1 occurs, however, when they lose sight of these goals as counseling proceeds. This can be compared to the runner who leaves the course halfway through the race. Clients frequently desire to "shift gears" to some extraneous complaint they may have recently experienced. Counselors swayed by personal voyeurism leave the main road. Counselors attuned to treatment goals offer clients the option of renegotiating the agreed-to goals. For example:

COUNSELOR: Your concerns about your friend Hank are relatively unrelated to your goal of completing tasks in a more timely manner. Is that goal still a priority for you or would you like to replace it with a goal related to your relationship with Hank?

Our experience is that when given the option of reprioritizing their goals, most clients put aside the immediate issue in favor of refocusing on their original goal. Should they choose to reprioritize their goals to address this immediate issue, however, this is fine, because the counseling will follow a new but still specific goal orientation.

Still other counselors contribute to counselor obstacle 1 by unilaterally setting the treatment goals. This typically occurs with counselors who tend to talk too much and request or even allow little client response. When clients are not invested in treatment goals, the probability of their working toward goal attainment is unlikely. Consider the following case illustration:

> A counselor was asked by two parents to assist them in developing better parenting skills with their three young children. The counselor suggested that it was the parents' marital relationship that needed to be in "good working order" before parenting practices could be addressed. The parents prematurely terminated after three subsequent sessions, during which the topic of their parenting practices was never raised.

Counselor obstacle 2 occurs when counselors mistakenly encourage clients to repeat unsuccessful solutions previously attempted. An area of inquiry for beginning counseling clients who report previous counseling experiences relates to those previous experiences in counseling: "What was beneficial for you during the counseling and what was not as beneficial for you?" For example:

CLIENT: I thought the counselor was a good listener. I had plenty of opportunity to get out the anger I was feeling. The problem was that we never seemed to go further than that. I think I needed more advice than was offered.

Understanding the client's view of previous counseling will provide critical information to help increase the likelihood of a successful outcome for present counseling efforts. Not having this knowledge could cause the counselor to repeat the past practice of another that was less effective than it might have been.

Counselor obstacle 2 also occurs when counselors repeat the same unsuccessful solutions that have brought the client to counseling. It is important to remember that responses 180 degrees toward the opposite direction of clients' typical solutions are desired. Repeating clients' unsuccessful solution attempts during the session or inadvertently suggesting that they do "more of the same" between sessions is a plan doomed for failure (O'Hanlon and Weiner-Davis, 1989). Consider the following case example:

A married couple came to counseling with the wife expressing the complaint that her husband "never shares what he's really feeling." After her introduction of the complaint, the counselor spent the next ten minutes trying to get the husband to describe how he felt about what the wife had just said. The husband said virtually nothing. The counselor felt at a loss.

In this case example, the wife readily described what was not working. The counselor rightfully sought to involve the husband in the counseling, but mistakenly did so in a way that was "more of the same" of what the wife had just reported as unsuccessful. An approach with a more helpful outcome might have been to move on with the wife to discuss exception times from her perspective. When the husband does share how he feels, even minimally, this could be reinforced. Thus, the opportunity to engage the husband in the counseling would be offered *by him,* and that would be a "different" solution.

Counselor obstacle 3 occurs when counselors focus on clients' complaints rather than on solutions. The most common contribution to this obstacle is introduced best by the well-known philosophical question "If a tree falls in a forest, and no one is there to hear it, is there any sound?" Similarly, reports of exception times, successful solutions, and client strengths and resources will dissipate quickly unless attended to. It is critical that counselors structure counseling sessions in such a manner that clients talk about exception times, more successful solutions, and their strengths and resources. It is also critical that counselors attend to this information so it is shared in such a way that conveys the message "This is important information for attaining your goal and resolving your complaint. Let's address it further."

In presenting their complaints some clients are most adamant about the nature and seriousness of their difficulties. Talking too much about complaints leads to thinking even more about the complaints, which leads to even further talking about the complaints. Unless complaints are talked about in new and different ways, they will likely be thought of in the same old way. If thinking about their complaints in the same old way was a successful solution, clients would not be clients. At these complaint-focused times, it is important that the counselor interrupt. This procedure can be compared to a courtroom attorney who objects to a line of questioning aimed at convincing the jury that there is no doubt about the client's guilt (O'Hanlon and Weiner-Davis, 1989). Consider the following case illustration:

CLIENT: I am just so depressed all the time. I awaken depressed and the day just seems to drag on. It's the same every day.

COUNSELOR A: It must be tough for you feeling so down all the time. What do you see yourself so depressed over?

COUNSELOR B: From my experience, I've come to understand that even the most depressed individuals find that the depression lifts a little for brief periods during the day so that they can get the essentials done. What do you do to recognize those more bearable times when you can attend to your daily needs?

Counselor A's response, although an expression of empathy, does little to convey to the client that hope for change is possible. Counselor B's response, by contrast, is solution-focused and conveys the idea that there are exception times; this subsequently provides a foundation upon which identification and amplification of more successful solutions can be pursued.

A final contribution to counselor obstacle 3 is the traditional concept of client resistance. We all occasionally attribute negative motivations to other persons' actions. To do so in counseling, however, can have serious ramifications. It is our belief and one affirmed by many "brief-oriented" counselors that client resistance is simply a label derived from traditional counseling approaches and given by counselors to clients when they reach an impasse. Unfortunately, labeling clients as resistant makes them antagonists rather than partners in the counseling process.

It is vital that time not be inefficiently spent battling with clients. Counselors who pay attention to the cooperative elements of the client-counselor relationship and build upon these more productive aspects experience more timely and successful movement toward therapeutic goal attainment. Focusing on these aspects of the interchange contributes to an environment in which a partnership facilitates the search for and implementation of more successful solutions. If clients have objections or are reluctant to follow some course of action, it is the counselor's responsibility to view these as legitimate concerns that need to be addressed in a solution-oriented, rather than problem-oriented, fashion by counselor and client together.

Ending Counseling Efforts

Until clients report their progress toward goal attainment (complaint resolution) as "better," the interval between sessions is typically a week or less. When counseling progress is assessed as "better enough," the interval between sessions is progressively lengthened—two weeks, then three weeks to a month. These intervals are used to communicate the message "Since things are going better, we need not get together so often" (that is, "You're employing more successful solutions, considering the more helpful rule more, and assuming a position of greater rationality").

In more traditional, lengthy approaches to counseling and psychotherapy, it is appropriate to regard ending counseling efforts—"termination"—as a special event. Over the course of time, a significant relationship develops between the client and counselor, and so the ending of counseling efforts is the ending of that relationship. Implicit in these approaches is the idea that treatment is aimed at far more than the resolution of specific complaints; rather, the counselor is assisting clients in gaining profound insights into themselves and their life circumstances. Thus, there is a sense of "cutting loose" from the importance and security of counseling, and counselors often prepare clients for termination, sometimes many weeks prior to the eventual last session (Fisch, Weakland, and Segal, 1982).

For the Twenty Minute Counselor, however, termination is not viewed as a special event. The brevity of counseling and the specific solution-oriented approach leave little time for "developing a relationship" between counselor and client; thus, there is little sense of having to pull away from the security of treatment or of cutting clients off to fend for themselves. A solution-oriented approach also delineates counseling as a means for better resolving specific complaints, so there is little need to spend significant time summarizing the accomplishments of counseling. From a brief counseling perspective, then, the handling of termination is, likewise, brief.

Three criteria tend to indicate the time for ending counseling efforts: (1) clients report that at least a small but significant change has occurred relative to the presenting complaint; (2) the change appears to be durable; and (3) clients imply or say that they can handle things on their own (Segal and Kahn, 1986). When it appears that the agreed-to goals have been attained, if the client does not say anything it is the counselor's role to ask the client whether or not it makes sense to end counseling efforts. Most of the time, clients will agree that it is time to terminate. Occasionally, some clients wish to recontract around a new issue, which is fine.

It is important that counselors highlight the notion that clients have accomplished what they set out to do, even when recontracting occurs. Clients often attribute the successful results of counseling efforts to the counselor: "I don't know how I could have gotten here without your help." While such gratitude is pleasing to receive, it puts the counselor in a one-up position and this can be a disadvantage to many clients when they terminate. It implicitly negates clients' own accomplishments and thereby defines clients as less in control of the events in their lives and more vulnerable to other, unforeseen difficulties. Although counselors cannot and should not stop clients from expressing their gratitude, they should nevertheless reframe the accomplishments of counseling so that clients leave in a one-up position. The simplest means of accomplishing this is by acknowledging clients' compliments but going on to reassert clients' own contributions to the success of counseling—the information they so succinctly offered, their willingness to try out different ways of thinking and acting, and so forth. Simultaneously, counselors should downgrade their own contribution: "It's a lot easier to be the 'Monday morning quarterback.'"

One major reason counselors have difficulty facilitating termination is that even when clients attain their expressed goal (resolve their presenting complaint), they can always offer details of further difficulties that they are experiencing—feeling down or angry, having a bad day at work or an argument with a spouse, child, or friend. We look at most of these as everyday examples of "downs," which constitute the ups and downs that are a natural part of living. The Twenty Minute Counselor seeks to enhance coping with recurrent difficulties. Brief therapy is not meant to be a panacea for all of life's challenges. As noted in the beginning of this book, one of our major focuses is "It's better to be living in the world than to be living in counseling."

7

Twenty Minutes with Couples and Families

The persons constituting a couple or a family system behave among themselves in organized, repetitive ways. These patterns of interaction can be abstracted as governing principles of marital and family life (Jackson, 1977). The Twenty Minute Counselor, when counseling with couples and families, thus tries to determine and address *patterns of interaction* (successful and unsuccessful solutions) and *governing principles* of marital and family life (rational and irrational rules).

Couples and family members are not necessarily aware of these commonly adhered to patterns and principles. For example, most marital and family rules are unwritten and covertly stated. They tend to be inferences that couples and family members make relative to the repetitive patterns they observe occurring around them. "Go to mother when you have a problem; she's more understanding." "It's best to ask father for money first thing in the morning when he's in a hurry to leave for work." A common family rule, unstated but understood by all, is that decisions are made by parents and handed down to children. Parents also learn and adhere to covert rules: the son is active in athletics, but it isn't something the daughter would enjoy; child A can be depended on to do well in school, but child B cannot; child C is not trustworthy with money, whereas child D is (Huber and Baruth, 1989). Consider the rule defining the following relationship between husband and wife as they prepare to go out for the evening:

WIFE: I wish you would update your clothes. I'd appreciate it if you'd pay greater attention to what you wear. Why don't you buy yourself a new suit?

HUSBAND: I just couldn't buy new clothes for myself when you and the kids need so many things.

WIFE: But we want you to do things for yourself too.

HUSBAND: I just couldn't put myself before all of you.

Contrary to initial appearances, the overt one-down behavior of the husband (wherein he places his needs "one down" from those of the rest of the family) is quite controlling. What sort of marital/family rule do they operate by? The wife is allowed to complain about her husband's appearance, but he retains control over the family's expenditure of money. He apparently does not intend to follow her suggestion and, moreover, cannot be faulted because he is the good person sacrificing for his family. This couple is thus stuck in a repetitive exchange of a more-of-the same solution in addressing their mutual circumstances.

The Twenty Minute Counselor uses the same basic understandings and session procedures counseling with couples and families as with individual clients. After a brief orientation to counseling from a twenty-minute framework, the counselor shifts focus to gather information on those elements important to the process at hand: the nature of the couple/family's complaint (reframed as desired goals), how the complaint is generally being unsuccessfully addressed (unsuccessful solutions), and "exception" times when the complaint has been more adequately addressed (successful solutions). This is followed by a contrasting of the unsuccessful solutions with the more successful solutions of the exception times in seeking a common denominator or "rule." The counselor concludes the session by amplifying previous successful efforts that have been unearthed (pretreatment changes) and reframing the "rule" in a more rational, helpful manner.

The major difference between counseling with individual clients and with couples or families is that with the latter, the Twenty Minute Counselor carefully attends to *marital/family frames of reference* as opposed to individual perceptions and beliefs. Commonly adhered to and acted out rules and solutions constitute these marital/family frames of reference. Likewise, the complaints considered and reframed as goals for counseling are also mutual ones.

The following transcription of a twenty-minute hour with a

married couple is offered here to illustrate the aforementioned focus on marital/family frames of reference. The couple have come to a local mental health facility with the hope of resolving some of the differences that threaten to undermine their relationship. The couple, Glenda and Ken, have been married for nineteen years. Glenda is a full-time homemaker, and Ken works with his father and two brothers in their local family business. They have four children, ages eighteen, twelve, eight, and five. The counselor is one of the authors (BAB).

The session begins with the counselor and couple discussing several consumer issues, including permission to tape-record the session. The following interaction starts immediately thereafter.

COUNSELOR: Glenda and Ken, why don't we begin by you helping me understand what it is that brings you both here and what you want to gain by coming to counseling. Ken, how about you?

KEN: Well, she says that I don't give enough time to her and the kids. When I come home from work . . . I work so hard . . . I like to sit down and have a beer and rest and get ready for the next day.

COUNSELOR: So you're pretty tired when you come home from work and it sounds like you'd like some time to unwind and that's become somewhat of a problem, getting that down time.

KEN: Yes, I'm real tired and I come home and Glenda has to start on me right when I walk in the door.

COUNSELOR: Glenda, how about you? Is that an area of major concern from how you see things?

GLENDA: You bet it is. I feel like he has time for everybody else and everything else outside of the house, like his work and then his friends. Then when he comes home to me and the kids . . . you know, we've been home all day. We love him and we miss him, and it's like he just hits the door and wants to be detached from us. That hurts me a lot and it hurts the kids a lot. We just want to be a family and I don't feel like he wants to be a family anymore. In a way, I feel like it's just a place that he comes home to rest.

COUNSELOR: So you and the kids have been home all day and you're excited about seeing him and maybe you're thinking, "I can't wait to share what I've been doing all day with him."

And, Ken, you come home and maybe you're thinking, "Oh, I can't wait to relax."

KEN: Yes. I need some alone time, to just step back and kind of unwind.

GLENDA: But why even have a family then? We only get in the way of—

KEN: Well, you all are important to me. It's just that my workdays are pretty rough sometimes.

GLENDA: I know that you work hard and I know that it's important that you make enough money to take care of us all, but I feel like what's it all for? I feel like it's really important for me to stay home and give the kids my time while they're younger. But basically, I quit working outside the home a long time ago to be with our children. Since then, we've some more and I feel that you have your whole life going on while I've just been at home with one kid after another. I just feel real left out.

COUNSELOR: Ken, would you respond to Glenda about what she just said. There are some pretty positive feelings as well as the not so positive being expressed there.

KEN: Like I said, I've been with people all day, dealing with customers' problems, and I really just want to be left alone for a little while. I don't want to talk about problems when I come home. I just want to sit down and relax, unwind, and you start bugging me to talk to you and listen to this or that problem— whatever's come up, kids, the washing machine. And when you start that, I just want to . . . withdraw. I just tune out. But I do love you and the kids and don't want us to have these arguments.

COUNSELOR: Glenda, it sounds like what you would like is for Ken to be more available to you when he comes home from work in the evenings. Ken, it doesn't sound like you don't want to talk with Glenda at all, just that you need some down time first.

KEN: Right. I mean, I love her. I want to spend time with her, with the kids. I just need some time to myself, and she doesn't seem to understand.

COUNSELOR: Perhaps a mutual goal for us to pursue here is to find a balance between the time you spend together and the time you spend alone. That way both of you can be more satisfied.

KEN: Well, yes, I'd like that. I'd like to get something settled about this.

GLENDA: I guess so, yes. I'd be willing to compromise if he just wouldn't ignore me so much.

The counselor ties Ken's and Glenda's individual complaints to a mutual goal from which both would gain if it were achieved. The goal of "balance" is somewhat vague. The counselor now seeks to help the couple be more concrete so that they can determine progress toward or attainment of the goal.

COUNSELOR: Glenda and Ken, what do you think you are going to be doing differently when you achieve that balance?

GLENDA: Well, I don't think there will be all the arguing and fighting—me demanding his time, him wanting to be alone.

KEN: That's right on. I'd love that.

A mutually acceptable goal has been arrived at and agreed upon. It has been made more concrete. The counseling now shifts to identify the couple's unsuccessful solutions and accompanying rule (remembering that it is a mutual marital frame of reference that will be emphasized).

COUNSELOR: I can't imagine that you both haven't already worked hard to find that balance of time in the evenings and to fight less as a result. Could you describe for me a specific evening when you both began with a relatively good attitude and good intentions and things just went sort of awry, as you've been describing, with Glenda demanding Ken's attention and Ken wanting to be left alone?

GLENDA: Pick any night. Last night.

COUNSELOR: Okay. Please tell me about last night and what each of you did.

GLENDA: He came home and I had been having some problems with the teenager and the two younger ones. Just the fact that I was having a lot of problems . . . I needed help with them. Plus some things around the house had gone wrong, the washer for one thing, plus some work that was supposed to have been done by some man that was not done, and I needed a lot of help. There were a lot of things that had gone on that day. And he tells me not to call him during work, so I don't.

He says, "Will you just keep it until I get home?" So I do, and when he gets home and I have these things to tell him and he doesn't want to hear about them, and he got very angry, the angriest he's ever been at me. He yelled at me right in front of the children. And I was just very upset and I told him that if he didn't take our marriage any more seriously than that, we were in big trouble. And I asked him to come in here today with me, because I could see that things are just getting worse.

KEN: And that's why I'm here. I don't want things to get any worse than they are.

COUNSELOR: So last night was paticularly bad for you too, Ken. How were you experiencing it, the details from your perspective?

KEN: I wasn't interested in hearing it. I wanted to relax and step back away from it all. She had things under control, she had control of the situation. I commend her for it. So I let her handle it. She always handles it and she does a good job.

COUNSELOR: So, Ken, you were thinking to yourself that Glenda would handle the problems with the children and house and there was no need for you to get involved. And, Glenda, you were thinking to yourself that you wanted to talk about the problems you were experiencing and you wanted Ken to listen. It sounds like the things you both did as a consequence left you both feeling angry and discouraged.

KEN: Yes.

GLENDA: Yes. I can't think of how to get what I want from him anymore. I'm shy about going to him with concerns. I just leave him alone as long as I can and when I get enough that I have to talk to him, well, then I talk to him and it just blows up.

COUNSELOR: With regard to last night at least, it seems to me that there was sort of an unspoken agreement, or maybe a spoken agreement, between the two of you—we might call it a "marital rule" that the two of you were operating under. It might have been something like, "It's Glenda's responsibility to handle the children and household problems and Ken's responsibility to work and support the family, and never the two should meet."

KEN: That's what I want her to do. Just handle it and leave me out of it. She always does.

GLENDA: Well, that's not what I want, but it sure seems to happen that way. That's not anything I agreed to.

COUNSELOR: And yet you acted on that belief. You handled things yourself and it appears would not have sought to involve Ken. However, yesterday seems to have been a real rough day.

GLENDA: Well, yes I do it. What choice do I have? He won't do it, somebody's got to. He won't deal with anything when he gets home. I'm always in the middle, taking care of stuff for him, keeping the kids away from him. Yes. I guess I do always do it.

The couple's unsuccessful solutions as described by them in the specific instance they offered were that Glenda assumed responsibility for the children and household, and Ken affirmed that she do so (both totally); and Ken assumed the responsibility for the financial support of the family, and Glenda affirmed that he do so (both totally). Although not explicitly stated, the actions of both partners confirm the existence of a marital rule contributing to these unsuccessful solutions: "and never the two should meet." It is important to note that it may not be the solutions themselves that are "bad," but rather the absolute and therefore irrational degree to which they are enacted makes the solutions unsuccessful.

The session now moves to an exception time and more successful solutions that the couple already have in their "solution repertoire."

COUNSELOR: It sounds like last evening is pretty typical of your evenings recently, given the complaints you've shared and the goal you've agreed to. Typical, however, isn't all the time. When was the last evening you both can remember that there was greater balance there, when you both had your desires met and did not argue?

GLENDA: Well, I've been feeling bad for some time. The last time I remember was about three weeks ago, Christmas vacation. They close the business down during the holiday week.

KEN: Yes. We had several nice evenings over Christmas.

COUNSELOR: Can you pick one evening during that week you might both recall. How about an evening in the middle of that week?

GLENDA: Christmas was on Monday this year, and I think it was Wednesday after Christmas. Ken had to go into the store, even though it was closed, to do some inventory work. The kids were all home from school with all their friends in and out and I wasn't feeling too well, kind of sick with the flu or something. I knew he was busy all day with the inventory, but I did call him and let him know I wasn't feeling well and when he came home could he take care of supper for himself and the kids. He was wonderful about doing so and I appreciated it so much. After supper, he came in and we laid in bed together just talking. It made me feel so good. The next day I was right up and about full steam.

KEN: It was kind of an unusual situation, being the holiday week and all. I didn't have to deal with customers all day. Doing the inventory was sort of relaxing, not rushed. I stopped on the way home and picked up some burgers and fries for us all for dinner. The McDonald's wasn't even that crowded and I remember not having to wait long for my rather large order.

COUNSELOR: Ken, it almost sounds like you had your alone time, your quiet time during the day at work, and some more during your drive home and stop at McDonald's. Glenda, it sounds like you still pretty much handled everything all day, but maybe it was easier knowing Ken would assume a small portion of the responsibilities, taking care of supper in this instance.

GLENDA: That's what made that whole week so nice. He just wasn't so tense and I think we did spend more time together. He came home and didn't just go off by himself. We were able to exchange some information during the day. I'd phone him since there were no customers he had to attend to and we'd just chat for a few moments. I didn't feel like he didn't want to listen. But it was Christmas vacation and the store was closed.

This interchange reflects how couples, like individual clients, have already-proven successful solutions in their "solution repertoire." The counselor need only elicit exception times that have gone unnoticed and appreciate their significance as a means of assisting the couple do so. As is typical, though, Ken and Glenda attribute their success to it occurring during Christmas vacation, not to their mutually acting and thinking differently toward each other and their complaint circumstances. The counselor follows this by facilitating a greater appreciation of their own involvement in the exception time; that is, how they specifically thought and acted differently.

COUNSELOR: You're right, it was Christmas vacation. The store was closed. But there were some problems that did arise—for example, your not feeling well, Glenda. How you both addressed them, particularly on that Wednesday evening, appears to be different from your earlier description of recent evenings. For example, you called Ken at work and warned him of your illness. You didn't ask him to spend time talking about problems, just that you needed some help when he came home. Ken, it sounds like you took care of your "alone time" needs before you came home and so when you came home you were more willing to lend a hand. And you both describe feeling very positive toward each other, leading to that intimate time together after dinner.

KEN: It was nice. It was real nice.

GLENDA: It was like falling in love again.

KEN: Well, it was nice to be at home. No fights. It's a shame it can't always be like that.

COUNSELOR: It's true that that was sort of an exception time, as you both see it. It was Christmas vacation. There were some things in your routines that were a bit different. Still, the two of you did things that had little to do with it being Christmas vacation. One thing that really sticks out to me is how you acted according to a somewhat different "marital rule" on that particular Wednesday evening and apparently the majority of that entire week. Instead of "Glenda takes total responsibility for the household and Ken takes total responsibility for financial support of the family *and never the two should meet,*" that last part changed to "and sometimes the two *can* meet."

The counselor, maintaining a therapeutic focus on rationality in her own thinking, was able to readily convey the idea that the couple's more successful solutions represented a change in direction for them 180 degrees toward a more rational, relative marital rule. The emphasis now in the session is to amplify the couple's consideration of their more rational, relative rule and, consequently, their use of already-proven successful accompanying solutions. Again, working with a couple or family, it is important to deal with the marital or family frame of reference—that rule they both adhere to, overtly if not covertly.

KEN: You know, it did seem to work better that way. I even liked helping out at home, being included. It wasn't that big of a deal to take care of supper.

COUNSELOR: And, Glenda, how about for you?

GLENDA: I was feeling more relaxed. I wasn't being so careful about everything I said and did. I guess I just felt more relaxed 'cause I felt that if something happened around the house it was okay to call him because the store was closed and he could help out if I absolutely needed him to. It was a relief not to be in a position where I felt I had to do it all myself.

COUNSELOR: So you're both saying that by changing your marital rule slightly to "and sometimes the two can meet" and acting accordingly, you both felt much better and got along much better; there were clearly fewer arguments. I wonder what this suggests to you about achieving the goal that you set at the beginning of our session today.

GLENDA: Well, it makes me think that maybe I am taking too much upon myself in relation to the household and kids. Perhaps I could offer some assistance to him at the store in exchange for some more assistance at home from him.

KEN: That's something we've never considered. I didn't know you had any interest in helping out at the store. I would really welcome it. But what about the house and kids?

GLENDA: If you were able to help with just supper a couple of nights, or didn't mind McDonald's or going out more often, I'd spend a couple of hours each week with the books. That would free you up more too, as you know you often bring them home to finish up with the posting. I also think I'd like getting out more.

COUNSELOR: There's still the issue of your desire for time to be alone and wind down after work, Ken. One successful solution that you described occurring over that Christmas vacation was getting some alone time *before* you came home in the evening, and so when you came home you were ready to interact with Glenda and the kids. How might you do that during the rest of the year, this week for example?

KEN: I could ask my dad or one of my brothers to close down the register and take care of the final customers while I finish the day's posting. I usually take it home to do after dinner. I find it kind of relaxing to compile the day's figures. There's no reason, though, that I couldn't spend the last thirty to forty-five minutes of my workday doing it in the back office alone.

COUNSELOR: That sounds like a superb solution. Glenda mentioned her willingness to help out with the books.

KEN: There're other accounting calculations that she could do apart from the posting. I'd really welcome not having to deal with those figures.

This latter interchange speaks strongly of the inherent strengths and resources of all persons. The couple's spontaneous generation of alternative solutions based on the more rational, relative marital rule is commendable.

COUNSELOR: You two are really rolling. I hate to stop us here, but our time is almost up. What I'd like to suggest is that we get together the same day and time next week just to review how well you're considering your marital rule of "and sometimes the two *should meet*" and putting that rule into action. Let's look at it as sort of a time to report back on your success and to iron out any final details if necessary. Five thirty next week.

GLENDA: Okay.

KEN: Okay.

When couples and families experience difficulties, there is often a tendency to perceive these difficulties as *happening to them* as opposed to a set of circumstances that each member contributes to. As in the above illustration with Ken and Glenda, by focusing on the "answer" for resolving their expressed difficulties as a solution that has already proven effective (the exception time), the counselor is able affirm their position and then assist them in expanding on it. Treatment is thus tailored to increasing their cooperation with each other and pursuing the agreed-upon counseling goals.

Individual and marital/family counseling approaches are often viewed at odds with each other. Counselors are either individually, intrapsychically oriented or they are interpersonally, systemically oriented. The Twenty Minute Counselor uses the same basic framework for working with individual clients and working with couples and families. The only difference is that the counselor working with couples and families affirms the position of the individual members but helps them expand on those individual positions in order to consider and act on the greater marital or family frame of reference.

8

Epilogue: More than a Treatment of Choice

Counseling within a twenty-minute hour framework is second nature to us now, but this hasn't always been the case. We both had our initial training in traditional, long-term counseling. The most difficult part of our evolution to the twenty-minute hour was letting go of the deeply ingrained idea that counseling is about exploring problems. We had to learn that instead of tuning into what was wrong with clients, our function as counselors is to assist them in finding the resources they already possess in order to move to more effective solutions. The key element in this process is defining the ambiguous concerns clients bring to counseling in manageable ways that elicit their own natural competence. When this is done with skill and sensitivity, the process of change can become breathtakingly sudden. One counselor's long-term client can be transformed into another's satisfied ex-client within a relatively short time (Weiner-Davis, 1990).

The work of one of us (CHH) with the Klingers (not their real name) illustrates this continuing process of evolutionary growth.

The Klingers are a highly successful family. The father is vice-president of a large insurance company, and the mother, a former professional social worker who left her career to devote full time to her family, is a "successful" mother and significant contributor to many major community efforts. Fifteen-year-old son Ned is a "gifted" student who excels in sports and academics. The Klingers also have two adopted children, eleven-year-old Mary and nine-year-old Jason, both doing fairly well given an early family-of-origin background of severe abuse.

Counseling was precipitated by a "suicide note" written by

Ned and accidently discovered by the father. Ned subsequently spoke with his parents and assured them that the note was only a reflection of some passing thoughts and he had absolutely no intention of suicidal action. The parents met with Ned and his school counselor, who confirmed Ned's assertions but referred the parents to me to address concerns they raised as a result.

I put to the family the question I ask all new clients: "What would you like to gain from counseling?" Although clients don't always provide me with answers to that question, opening our time together in this manner sends the message that I assume there is something they want to gain—a goal—and that achieving their goal will be the focus of our time together.

"We've failed as parents. How could our son even think of killing himself!" was the parents' reply. Immediately, several warning flares went up. I recognized the temptation to take the pathology route and pick up on that classic bugaboo—overinvolved, enmeshed parents—and analyze extensively whatever was wrong with the family interaction. But knowing what to ignore has become one of my most important counseling skills. I had been offered a potentially negative image of the family that I could reinforce by discussing it further, or I could look beyond the pessimism and find a way to work with them based on their strengths.

As I continued to listen, the depressing statistics about adolescent suicide echoed in my mind. Quickly dismissing this temporary distraction, I thought instead of excerpts from the family life cycle literature suggesting that this time of their family life was potentially tumultuous for the Klingers, but equally full of potential for evolutionary growth. I knew it was time to intervene.

"When did you decide you wanted to be different as parents?" I asked.

"Just this past week when we discovered the suicide note," replied both parents.

The parents' few words provided me with enough information to begin to alter their negative, irrational, absolutistic view of their circumstances. I emphatically responded, "So up until this past week, you've been doing a reasonably acceptable job as parents. That certainly changes things." The parents looked puzzled. "After all," I reassured them, "for the past how many years you've managed to do some pretty successful parenting. Now you've encountered a significant roadblock and are immediately addressing it in a most appropriate manner, as successful parents would."

I carefully watched for their response. Were they clients who would feel supported and encouraged by this kind of feedback, or would they let me know in some way that I was missing the boat? Quiet for a moment, they both reported how they had felt very good about their parenting and were caught completely unaware by Ned's note. I was relieved and encouraged by how readily these parents saw themselves in a less negative, more rational and relative light. We were already chiseling away at their hopeless view of their situation. A few moments before, they had seen themselves as failures as parents. Now they saw themselves as having only recently encountered a roadblock after a history of successful parenting. Although this rapid shift, within only a few minutes, to seeing problems as more manageable happens with great regularity in my practice, it still feels like magic to me, as it did that day with the Klingers.

I had an idea about the Klingers. They could not have been so successful in business and community efforts without considerable human relations skills, and this had likely been part of the basis for their previous parenting successes. I asked, "If you were asked for assistance by a colleague or subordinant experiencing a seemingly terrible dilemma in your business or community life, how would you respond to that person?" The parents looked out in space and were silent for several moments. I was afraid that they would reject outright my suggestion that they possess their own resources for resolving their dilemma. Instead, they admitted that they had discussed how to deal with Ned's note and tentatively agreed on a plan. Although somewhat embarrassed that they approached their son like a professional objective, with my reassurance they revealed the details of their strategy.

"Well, we decided that we have taken Ned for granted for some time. Since we adopted Mary and Jason, we've had to devote the major portion of our attention to them. Their abused backgrounds made their assimilation into the family a slow and arduous one. And Ned has been great about it; never a complaint or jealous word." The father used the analogy of Ned being like an insurance client who happily has been paying his premiums but is filing a claim and needs to be attended to more directly as a consequence. The mother compared Ned to several of the workers at the publicly funded day care center, on whose Board of Directors she serves. Overworked and underpaid, they did their job diligently, but burnout had taken its toll until the board took steps to attend more directly to their needs.

Research has indicated that between the initial call for a counseling appointment and the first session, over two-thirds of clients have already taken specific steps to improve their circumstances. So the Klingers' actions did not surprise me.

As they went on to describe their "professional strategy," their self-confidence and determination were evident. My reinforcing the link between their business and community competence and their success as parents was probably the turning point in the counseling.

At the end of that first session, I gave them lots of positive feedback, suggested that they look for signs that they were continuing on the right track, and set a time to get together again in two weeks. I felt that since they had a specific plan, all they needed was the time to implement it. But when, only five days later, father called asking if we could meet sooner, I became apprehensive and wondered whether I had misjudged the situation.

When they came to the session, I was prepared for the worst. Although I felt like asking, "What went wrong?" I instead opened on a positive note: "I'm very much looking forward to hearing about how well your strategy went with Ned." Both offered smiles, which surprised me. "We've had a great week. The reason we wanted to get together is that we wanted to bounce some ideas off of you." I was delighted and thankful that I relied on my belief that clients' natural competence need only be highlighted for positive change to occur. In the weeks that followed, their increased attention to Ned bore fabulous fruit. A phone check with the family six months after their initial contact found all going well. In fact, Ned was communicating regularly and intimately with his parents as a consequence of their increased attention to him.

As we reflect back on our days doing longer-term counseling, and how long and hard we worked to help clients reach the same point the Klingers reached in two brief sessions, we find it hard to believe, like many of the supervisees and students we train, that doing successful counseling can be so easy. I never discussed with the Klingers why they felt like failures or how those feelings developed. I knew little about their family background or the details of their previous parenting efforts. My major focus in initial efforts was identifying that the Klingers had a goal that they believed, for some reason, they were unable to accomplish. My seeing them as capable and resourceful brought out their innate capability and resourcefulness. For us, the primary challenge of counseling is using all our skills and understanding to assist clients see that they are the experts on their lives. They have the solutions. We need only ask the right questions.

Of course, not all clients respond as readily as the Klingers did. Counselors we supervise and students we train frequently comment on how speedily we seek to shift from complaints to goals to new alternative solutions. They seem to come full of traditional psychodynamic ideas, including the need for more extensive history taking, for allowing clients to ventilate, for lengthy rapport building, and for in-depth personality reconstruction. To be sure, there are many clients who present with significantly greater adherence to their complaint times over exceptions times than the Klingers. We respect their position. We go along with their desire to ventilate their distressful feelings, to tell more of their story. We go further, however, and work to expand their position. As we are open to clients, they become more open to us.

For example, consider clients and counselors in some future "perfect world," like that described by Manaster (1989):

> If there were a need for therapy at all in a perfect world, that therapy could be elaborated and extended for thoroughness, completeness, and the pleasure of unconditional reflection and introspection. Case studies, popular wisdom, and clinical experience show us that many, if not all, patients would be content with this process, if they could afford the time and money. And why not? To focus on oneself, to be the center of one's own and someone else's attention, in the interest of becoming a better person, with no pressure to change, allows one to accept and maintain a problem without guilt and with an everpresent excuse to oneself and others for not changing or improving. (P. 245)

The Twenty Minute Counselor would advocate that counselors accept, but then go further and work to expand, clients' position in that future perfect world, to point out that counseling in a perfect world should *also* be efficient as well as effective. And in our imperfect world, do persons entering counseling not seek the earliest possible relief from their distress and the means to maintain a more satisfying and enriching life-style? The Twenty Minute Counselor asserts that counselors have an ethical and moral responsibility to effect clients' increased well-being as efficiently and effectively as possible.

Is it possible to promote positive client change in a single twenty-minute session? We would assert yes. Need the pivotal interaction in counseling occur in the fortieth session as opposed to the fourteenth, the fourth, or the first? It need not. Can we clearly confirm when it will occur? In this imperfect world, we can only know, with limited confidence, that change will not occur until late in a lengthy counseling process, if counselors act on the belief that it will be that way (Manaster, 1989). If counselors do not work to promote change early in the process—if they convey to clients a belief that nothing substantial will occur for a long time—they will more often than not be proven correct.

This is especially true with clients given a diagnosis that has historically been shown, or thought, to be exceptionally difficult to treat. O'Hanlon's (1990) thoughts are most apt on this issue:

> Whenever I give workshops on brief therapy, someone usually gets up and asks, "But what about borderlines? Does this brief therapy stuff work on them?" The question strikes right to the heart of the differences between most brief therapists and their long-term therapy colleagues. Brief therapists typically see the client's presenting problem as negotiable. We focus on changeable aspects of people's lives and on clear obtainable results . . . borderline personality disorders are not on the brief therapy menu. I should also add that they are not on most clients' menus either. (P. 48)

Clients don't come seeking counseling for their personality disorders unless they have learned the label from some therapist or from the media. We don't advocate attending to personality diagnoses. How often is the term *ordered personality* employed?

The answer to that question ("Virtually never!") offers a cogent commentary on pursuing such an illusive therapeutic objective.

Throughout this book, we have emphasized a belief in the uniqueness of each client and the uniqueness of the ways in which clients find themselves "stuck" in vicious cycles of "more of the same" unsuccessful solutions framed by the irrational rules they rigidly adhere to. Fewer and fewer of our clients have expressed desires to ventilate more, to tell more of the grueling details of their difficulties. More and more of our counseling efforts are effective and brief because we act on the belief that positive change can occur for anyone at any time and we work to promote that change sooner rather than later. We make clear our intentions to do brief, efficient, effective counseling and thus attempt to make every counseling encounter a "therapeutic whole."

This is not to say that all of our counseling efforts are brief twenty-minute sessions. Although most now are, when we are not successful, we don't rigidly hold to a "more of the same" philosophy. We move toward the opposite direction: longer and/ or more sessions. We cannot, however, think of a moral or ethical justification for spending a long time counseling a client when a shorter time will suffice. There is no reason to believe that anything will be lost when counseling is begun with brief-ness as its focus and then extended in length of sessions and number of sessions as necessary. It is thus our contention that the twenty-minute hour is more than the treatment of choice. It is the treatment for all cases and all clients. And if a client's counseling experience does by necessity extend past the time defined as "brief," it should still continue only for the briefest time possible to attain the agreed-to counseling goals.

References

Andreas, C., and S. Andreas. 1990. Briefer than brief. *Family Therapy Networker* 14(2): 36–41.

Bateson, G. 1979. *Mind and nature: A necessary unit.* New York: Dutton.

Beck, A. T., A. J. Rush, B. F. Shaw, and G. Emery. 1978. *Cognitive therapy of depression: A treatment manual.* Unpublished.

Beutler, L., and M. Crago. 1987. Strategies and techniques of prescriptive psychotherapeutic intervention. In *Psychiatric updates: The American Psychiatric Association annual review,* ed. R. Hales and A. Frances. Washington, D.C.: American Psychiatric Press.

Bloom, B. 1981. Focused single-session therapy: Initial developments and evaluation. In *Forms of brief therapy,* ed. S. Budman. New York: Guilford.

Budman, S., and A. Gurman. 1983. The practice of brief therapy. *Professional Psychology* 14: 272–92.

Butcher, J., and M. Koss. 1978. Research in brief and crisis-oriented therapy. In *Handbook of psychotherapy and behavior change,* ed. S. Garfield and A. Bergin. New York: John Wiley.

de Shazer, S. 1982. *Patterns of brief family therapy.* New York: Guilford.

———. 1985. *Keys to solution in brief therapy.* New York: Norton.

———. 1988. *Clues: Investigating solutions in brief therapy.* New York: Norton.

de Shazer, S., J. K. Berg, E. Lipchik, E. Nunnally, A. Molnar, W. Gingerich, and M. Weiner-Davis. 1986. Brief therapy: Focused solution development. *Family Process* 25: 207–21.

de Shazer, S., and A. Molnar. 1984. Four useful interventions in brief family therapy. *Journal of Marital and Family Therapy* 10: 297–304.

DiGiuseppe, R., and C. Zeeve. 1985. Rational-emotive couples counseling. In *Clinical applications of rational-emotive therapy,* ed. A. Ellis and M. E. Bernard. New York: Plenum.

Dryden, W. 1984. *Rational-emotive therapy: Fundamentals and innovations.* London: Croom Helm.

Ellis, A. 1971. Emotional disturbance and its treatment in a nutshell. *Canadian Counselor* 5: 168–71.

———. 1978. Toward a theory of personality. In *Readings in current personality theories*, ed. R. J. Corsini. Itasca, Ill.: Peacock.

———. 1979. The theory of rational-emotive therapy. In *Theoretical and empirical foundations of rational-emotive therapy*, ed. A. Ellis and J. M. Whiteley. Monterey, Calif.: Brooks/Cole.

———. 1980. Rational-emotive therapy and cognitive behavior therapy: Similarities and differences. *Cognitive Therapy and Research* 4: 325–40.

———. 1982. Rational-emotive family therapy. In *Family counseling and therapy*, ed. A. M. Horne and M. M. Ohlsen. Itasca, Ill.: Peacock.

———. 1987. The impossibility of achieving consistently good mental health. *American Psychologist* 42: 364–75.

Emerson, R. T., and S. L. Messinger. 1977. The micro-politics of trouble. *Social Problems* 25: 121–34.

Fiester, A., and K. Rudestan. 1975. A multivariate analysis of the early treatment dropout process. *Journal of Consulting and Clinical Psychology* 43: 528–35.

Fisch, R., J. Weakland and L. Segal. 1982. *The tactics of change: Doing therapy briefly*. San Francisco: Jossey-Bass.

Garfield, S. 1986. Research on client variables in psychotherapy. In *Handbook of psychotherapy and behavior change*, ed. S. Garfield and A. Bergin. New York: John Wiley.

Goldenberg, I., and H. Goldenberg. 1980. *Family therapy: An overview.* Monterey, Calif.: Brooks/Cole.

Huber, C. H., and L. G. Baruth. 1989. *Rational-emotive family therapy: A systems perspective.* New York: Springer.

Jackson, D. 1977. The study of the family. In *The interactional view*, ed. P. Watzlawick and J. Weakland. New York: Norton.

McPherson, S. R., W. E. Brackelmanns, and L. E. Newman. 1974. Stages in the family therapy of adolescents. *Family Process* 13: 77–94.

Manaster, G. J. 1989. Clinical issues in brief psychotherapy: A summary and conclusion. *Individual Psychology: The Journal of Adlerian Theory, Research and Practice* 45: 243–47.

Minuchin, S., and H. C. Fishman. 1981. *Family therapy techniques.* Cambridge, Mass.: Harvard University Press.

O'Hanlon, W. H. 1990. Debriefing myself. *Family Therapy Networker* 14(2): 48–49, 68–69.

O'Hanlon, W. H., and M. Weiner-Davis. 1989. *In search of solutions.* New York: Norton.

Perry, S. 1987. The choice of duration and frequency for out-patient psychotherapy. In *Psychiatric update: The American Psychiatric Association annual review*, ed. R. Hales and A. Frances. Washington, D.C.: American Psychiatric Press.

Phillips, E. 1985. *Psychotherapy revised: New frontiers in research and practice*. Hillsdale, N.J.: Lawrence Erlbaum Associates.

Schorer, C. E., P. Lowinger, T. Sullivan, and G. H. Hartlaub. 1968. Improvement without treatment. *Diseases of the Nervous System* 29: 100–104.

Segal, L., and J. Kahn. 1986. Brief family therapy. *Individual Psychology: The Journal of Adlerian Theory, Research and Practice* 42: 545–55.

Sperry, L. 1989. Contemporary approaches to brief psychotherapy. *Individual Psychology: The Journal of Adlerian Theory, Research, and Practice* 45: 3–23.

Spivack, G., J. Platt, and M. Shure. 1976. *The problem-solving approach to adjustment*. San Francisco: Jossey-Bass.

Walen, S., R. DiGiuseppe, and R. Wessler. 1980. *A practitioner's guide to rational-emotive therapy*. New York: Oxford University Press.

Watzlawick, P., J. Weakland, and R. Fisch. 1974. *Change: Principles of problem formation and problem resolution*. New York: Norton.

Webster's new collegiate dictionary. 1976. Springfield, Mass. G. & C. Merriam.

Weiner-Davis, M. 1990. In praise of solutions. *Family Therapy Networker* 14(2): 42–48.

Weiner-Davis, M., S. de Shazer, and W. J. Gingerich. 1987. Building on pretreatment change to construct the therapeutic solution: An exploratory study. *Journal of Marital and Family Therapy* 13: 359–63.

Wessler, R., and R. Wessler. 1980. *The principles and practice of rational-emotive therapy*. San Francisco: Jossey-Bass.

THE CONTINUUM
COUNSELING LIBRARY
Books of Related Interest

_____Denyse Beaudet
ENCOUNTERING THE MONSTER
Pathways in Children's Dreams
Based on original empirical research, and with recourse to the
works of Jung, Neumann, Eliade, Marie-Louise Franz, and
others, this book offers proven methods of approaching and
understanding the dream life of children. $17.95

_____Robert W. Buckingham
CARE OF THE DYING CHILD
A Practical Guide for Those Who Help Others
"Buckingham's book delivers a powerful, poignant message
deserving a wide readership."—*Library Journal* $17.95

_____Alastair V. Campbell, ed.
A DICTIONARY OF PASTORAL CARE
Provides information on the essentials of counseling and the
kinds of problems encountered in pastoral practice. The approach is interdenominational and interdisciplinary. Contains
over 300 entries by 185 authors in the fields of theology, philosophy, psychology, and sociology as well as from the theoretical
background of psychotherapy and counseling. $24.50

_____David A. Crenshaw
BEREAVEMENT
Counseling the Grieving throughout the Life Cycle
Grief is examined from a life cycle perspective, infancy to old
age. Special losses and practical strategies for frontline
caregivers highlight this comprehensive guidebook. $16.95

_____Reuben Fine
THE HISTORY OF PSYCHOANALYSIS
New Expanded Edition
"Objective, comprehensive, and readable. A rare work. Highly
recommended, whether as an introduction to the field or as a
fresh overview to those already familiar with it."—*Contemporary
Psychology* $24.95 paperback

_____Reuben Fine
LOVE AND WORK
The Value System of Psychoanalysis
One of the world's leading authorities on Freud sheds new light
on psychoanalysis as a process for releasing the power of love.
$24.95

_____Raymond B. Flannery, Jr.
BECOMING STRESS-RESISTANT
Through the Project SMART Program
"An eminently practical book with the goals of helping men and
women of the 1990s make changes in their lives."—Charles V.
Ford, Academy of Psychosomatic Medicine $17.95

_____Lucy Freeman
FIGHT AGAINST FEARS
With a new Introduction by
Flora Rheta Schreiber
More than a million copies sold. The new—and only available—
edition of the first, and still best, true story of a modern woman's
journey of self-discovery through psychoanalysis.
$10.95 paperback

_____Lucy Freeman
OUR INNER WORLD OF RAGE
Understanding and Transforming the Power of Anger
A psychoanalytic examination of the anger that burns within us
and which can be used to save or slowly destroy us. Sheds light
on all expressions of rage, from the murderer to the suicide to
those of us who feel depressed and angry but are unaware of the
real cause. $9.95 paperback

_____ John Gerdtz and Joel Bregman, M. D.
AUTISM
A Practical Guide for Those Who Help Others
An up-to-date and comprehensive guidebook for everyone who
works with autistic children, adolescents, adults, and their
families. Includes latest information on medications. $17.95

_____Marion Howard
HOW TO HELP YOUR TEENAGER
POSTPONE SEXUAL INVOLVEMENT
Based on a national educational program that works, this book
advises parents, teachers, and counselors on how they can help
their teens resist social and peer pressures regarding sex.
$9.95 paperback

_____Marion Howard
SOMETIMES I WONDER ABOUT ME
Teenagers and Mental Health
Combines fictional narratives with sound, understandable
professional advice to help teenagers recognize the difference
between serious problems and normal problems of adjustment.
$9.95

_____Charles H. Huber and Barbara A. Backlund
THE TWENTY MINUTE COUNSELOR
Transforming Brief Conversations into Effective
Helping Experiences
Expert advice for anyone who by necessity must often counsel
"on the run" or in a short period of time. $16.95

_____E. Clay Jorgensen
CHILD ABUSE
A Practical Guide for Those Who Help Others
Essential information and practical advice for caregivers called
upon to help both child and parent in child abuse. $16.95

_____Eugene Kennedy ·
CRISIS COUNSELING
The Essential Guide for Nonprofessional Counselors
"An outstanding author of books on personal growth selects
types of personal crises that our present life-style has made
commonplace and suggests effective ways to deal with them."
—*Best Sellers* $10.95

_____Eugene Kennedy and Sara Charles, M. D.
ON BECOMING A COUNSELOR
A Basic Guide for Nonprofessional Counselors
New expanded edition of an indispensable resource. A patient-
oriented, clinically directed field guide to understanding and
responding to troubled people. $27.95 hardcover
$15.95 paperback

_____Eugene Kennedy
SEXUAL COUNSELING
A Practical Guide for Those Who Help Others
Newly revised and up-to-date edition, with a new chapter on
the counselor and AIDS, of an essential book on counseling
people with sexual problems. $17.95

_____Bonnie Lester
WOMEN AND AIDS
A Practical Guide for Those Who Help Others
Provides positive ways for women to deal with their fears, and
to help others who react with fear to people who have AIDS.
$15.95

_____Robert J. Lovinger
RELIGION AND COUNSELING
The Psychological Impact of Religious Belief
How counselors and clergy can best understand the important
emotional significance of religious thoughts and feelings. $17.95

_____Helen B. McDonald and Audrey I. Steinhorn
HOMOSEXUALITY
A Practical Guide to Counseling Lesbians, Gay Men, and Their Families
A sensitive guide to better understanding and counseling gays, lesbians, and their parents, at every stage of their lives. $17.95

_____ James McGuirk and Mary Elizabeth McGuirk
FOR WANT OF A CHILD
A Psychologist and His Wife Explore the Emotional Effects and Challenges of Infertility
A new understanding of infertility that comes from one couple's lived experience, as well as sound professional advice for couples and counselors. $17.95

_____ Janice N. McLean and Sheila A. Knights
PHOBICS AND OTHER PANIC VICTIMS
A Practical Guide for Those Who Help Them
"A must for the phobic, spouse and family, and for the physician and support people who help them. It can spell the difference between partial therapy with partial results and comprehensive therapy and recovery." — Arthur B. Hardy, M. D., Founder, TERRAP Phobia Program $15.95

_____ John B. Mordock and William Van Ornum
CRISIS COUNSELING WITH CHILDREN AND ADOLESCENTS
A Guide for Nonprofessional Counselors
New Expanded Edition
"Every parent should keep this book on the shelf right next to the nutrition, medical, and Dr. Spock books."—*Marriage & Family Living* $12.95

_____ John B. Mordock
COUNSELING CHILDREN
Basic Principles for Helping the Troubled and Defiant Child
Helps counselors consider the best route for a particular child,
and offers proven principles and methods to counsel troubled
children in a variety of situations. $17.95

_____ Cherry Boone O'Neill
DEAR CHERRY
Questions and Answers on Eating Disorders
Practical and inspiring advice on eating disorders from the best-
selling author of *Starving for Attention.* $8.95

_____ Paul G. Quinnett
ON BECOMING A HEALTH
AND HUMAN SERVICES MANAGER
A Practical Guide for Clinicians and Counselors
A new and essential guide to management for everyone in the
helping professions—from mental health to nursing, from social
work to teaching. $19.95

_____ Paul G. Quinnett
SUICIDE: THE FOREVER DECISION
For Those Thinking About Suicide,
and For Those Who Know, Love, or Counsel Them
"A treasure— this book can help save lives. It will be especially
valuable not only to those who are thinking about suicide but to
such nonprofessional counselors as teachers, clergy, doctors,
nurses, and to experienced therapists."—William Van Ornum,
psychotherapist and author $18.95 hardcover $8.95 paperback

_____ Paul G. Quinnett
WHEN SELF-HELP FAILS
A Consumer's Guide to Counseling Services
A guide to professional therapie. "Without a doubt one of the
most honest, reassuring, nonpaternalistic, and useful self-help
books ever to appear."—*Booklist* $10.95

_____ Judah L. Ronch
ALZHEIMER'S DISEASE
A Practical Guide for Those Who Help Others
Must reading for everyone who must deal with the effects of this tragic disease on a daily basis. Filled with examples as well as facts, this book provides insights into dealing with one's feelings as well as with such practical advice as how to choose long-term care. $11.95 paperback

_____Theodore Isaac Rubin, M. D.
ANTI-SEMITISM : A DISEASE OF THE MIND
"A most poignant and lucid psychological examination of a severe emotional disease. Dr. Rubin offers hope and understanding to the victim and to the bigot. A splendid job!"
—Dr. Herbert S. Strean $14.95

_____Theodore Isaac Rubin, M.D.
CHILD POTENTIAL
Fulfilling Your Child's Intellectual, Emotional, and Creative Promise
Information, guidance, and wisdom—a treasury of fresh ideas for parents to help their children become their best selves without professional help. $17.95

_____ John R. Shack
COUPLES COUNSELING
A Practical Guide for Those Who Help Others
An essential guide to dealing with the 20 percent of all counseling situations that involve the relationship of two people. $17.95

_____Stuart Sutherland
THE INTERNATIONAL DICTIONARY OF PSYCHOLOGY
This new dictionary of psychology also covers a wide range of related disciplines, from anthropology to sociology. $49.95

_____ Joan Leslie Taylor
IN THE LIGHT OF DYING
The Journals of a Hospice Volunteer
A rare and beautiful book about death and dying that affirms life
and will inspire an attitude of love. "Beautifully recounts the
healing (our own) that results from service to others, and might
well be considered as required reading for hospice volunteers."
—Stephen Levine, author of *Who Dies?* $17.95

_____Montague Ullman, M. D. and Claire Limmer, M. S., eds.
THE VARIETY OF DREAM EXPERIENCE
Expanding Our Ways of Working With Dreams
"Lucidly describes the beneficial impact dream analysis can have
in diverse fields and in society as a whole. An erudite, illuminat-
ing investigation."—*Booklist*
$19.95 hardcover $14.95 paperback

_____William Van Ornum and Mary W. Van Ornum
TALKING TO CHILDREN ABOUT NUCLEAR WAR
"A wise book. A needed book. An urgent book."
—Dr. Karl A. Menninger $15.95 hardcover $7.95 paperback

_____Kathleen Zraly and David Swift, M. D.
ANOREXIA, BULIMIA, AND COMPULSIVE OVEREATING
A Practical Guide for Counselors and Families
A psychiatrist and an eating disorders specialist provide new
and helpful approaches for everyone who knows, loves, or
counsels victims of anorexia, bulimia, and chronic overeating.
$17.95

At your bookstore, or to order directly, send your check or
money order (adding $2.00 extra per book for postage and
handling, up to $6.00 maximum) to: The Continuum Publishing
Company, 370 Lexington Avenue, New York, NY , 10017. Prices
are subject to change.